Presented to:

_____

Presented by:

_____

Date:

_____

Life's Simple Guide to Happiness: Inspirational Insights for Experiencing True Joy
Copyright © 2007 Bordon-Winters LLC

Product developed by Bordon Books, Tulsa, Oklahoma.
Concept: David Bordon and Tom Winters
Project Writing: Rebecca Currington, Kathryn Deering, Lisa Freeman, Vickie Phelps, and Robin Schmitt in association with SnapdragonGroup^sm Editorial Services.
Design by Greg Jackson, Thinkpen Design

FaithWords
Hachette Book Group USA
1271 Avenue of the Americas
New York, NY 10020

Visit our Web site at www.faithwords.com

The FaithWords name and logo are trademarks of Hachette Book Group USA.

Printed in the United States of America.
First Edition: August 2007
10 9 8 7 6 5 4 3 2 1
ISBN 10: 0-446-57938-6
ISBN 13: 978-0-446-57938-4

LCCN: 2006938653

Life's
Simple Guide to
HAPPINESS

Inspirational Insights for Experiencing True Joy

David Bordon and Tom Winters

New York Boston Nashville

INTRODUCTION

Happiness—so simple and yet, so elusive. Some people strive for it all their lives and never find it, believing that if they work hard enough, get enough lucky breaks, meet the right people, and find the right job, happiness will become a reality for them. Typically, they find that with time, they grow older—but rarely happier.

Is there a secret to happiness? In fact there is! That secret is hidden in plain sight. It is the eternal theme of the most popular book ever written—the Bible. *Life's Simple Guide to Happiness: Inspirational Tips for Experiencing True Joy* was designed to expose the secrets to be found in that magnificent book.

You may be surprised to see how practical, how commonplace those secrets are. Certainly, they often contradict the conventional wisdom of many happiness gurus. But they line up perfectly with God's plan for those who seek and find Him. Read it with your heart as well as your head, and you may well become one of those fortunate people everyone admires—a happy person!

CONTENTS

Life's

SIMPLE GUIDE TO

HAPPINESS

If you want to be happy, be.

ALEXEI TOLSTOY

TAKE A LOOK AROUND YOU.

Since the creation of the world God's invisible qualities—his eternal
power and divine nature—have been clearly seen, being understood
from what has been made, so that men are without excuse.

ROMANS 1:20

Our heavenly Father has given us a big, bright, wonderful
world with an infinite number of opportunities for happiness.
All we need to do is take a break from the frenetic business of life
and look around.

Just to illustrate this point, glance outside your window at
the trees in your yard. See them in a way you haven't before—as
unique creations, boasting of God's artistic talent and constant
care. Notice the lines of the trunks and the configurations of the
branches. If your trees are wearing flowering buds or promising
fruit, allow yourself to rejoice in the miracle of life begetting life.
If your tree is soaking up the rain—each leaf grabbing hold of
the drops—rest happily in the knowledge that God continues
to sustain His handiwork. If your tree is covered with a fluffy
blanket of snow, remind yourself that God has covered all His
creation with His love.

When you've tired of studying the trees, move on to the
flowers, plants, birds, animals—both great and small—oceans

bright and mountain splendor. Lift your eyes to the sky to see white puffy clouds dotting a tranquil blue canopy or rolling gray-black in a powerful display of God's sovereignty. It's a never-ending God-scape, just waiting for your eyes to behold it.

Happiness is not something that happens to you. It's something that surrounds you every day of your life. Happiness is being able to see God's artwork whenever you want. Open your eyes and take it all in. It's His gift to you.

SIMPLY SPEAKING

Think of the number of trees and blades of grass and flowers, the extravagant wealth of beauty no one ever sees! Think of the sunrises and sunsets we never look at! God is lavish in every degree.

OSWALD CHAMBERS

☺ LIVING THE HAPPY LIFE

Try spending some time outdoors today, soaking in the beauty of God's creation.

TAKE CARE OF YOUR BODY.

Dear friend, I pray that you may enjoy good health and that all may
go well with you, even as your soul is getting along well.

3 JOHN 2

In an average day, your body spontaneously performs—give
or take a little for age, size, and gender—all of the following
tasks:

- You exercise 7 million brain cells.
- Your heart beats 103,689 times.
- Your hair grows .01717 of an inch.
- Your blood travels 168,000,000 miles.
- Your nails grow .000046 of an inch.
- You move 750 major muscles.
- You inhale 438 cubic feet of air.
- You speak 48,000 words.
- You eat 3.25 pounds of food.
- You turn in your sleep 25–30 times.
- You drink 2.9 pounds of liquids.
- You give off 85.6 degrees Farenheit of heat.
- You perspire 1.43 pints!

Add to that remarkable list the things you will your body
to do each day. No doubt about it, your soul is being housed at

present in magnificent surroundings. How well do you take care of this gift God has given you? Your happiness quotient depends on your doing all you can.

Remember that when you're tempted to break your diet, forego your exercise program, skip your doctor's visit, or place yourself in harm's way. A strong, healthy body can provide a lifetime of happiness. Make sure you take care of your greatest earthly asset.

SIMPLY SPEAKING 📢

The body is matter, but it is God's creation. When it is neglected or scoffed at, God himself is insulted.

MICHEL QUOIST

☺ LIVING THE HAPPY LIFE

If you haven't done so in a while, make an appointment for a complete physical. You won't regret it!

FIND A CHURCH HOME.

Let us not give up meeting together, as some are in the habit of doing, but let us encourage one another—and all the more as you see the Day approaching.

HEBREWS 10:25

One of the secrets of being happy is to place yourself in an environment that nurtures the elements of happiness. One such place exists within the community of believers—your local church.

A church home provides its members with a sense of belonging, an opportunity to experience life with others, and the assurance that our time here on earth has meaning and significance. These elements nourish our souls in the same way sunlight, water, and nutrients sustain a plant and produce an abundance of colorful blossoms.

Perhaps you don't know where to find such a place. Take a drive near your home and note the established churches in your area. The religion section of your local newspaper often gives service times and a calendar of events. If the church you're interested in isn't listed there, look in your phone directory for the number and call the church office. This will give you an opportunity to ask about the size of the congregation, activities, service times, as well as other questions you might have.

The next step is to visit a service to get a sense of the church's personality. Is the congregation older or made up mostly of young families with children? Is the music spontaneous and joyful or deeply moving and liturgical? You're looking for something that best fits your personal lifestyle and comfort level.

Listen carefully to the pastor's sermon. Is it relevant to your life? Are the people friendly and open? Do you sense God's presence there?

God wants to help you find just the right place—a home where fellow believers can help you live, laugh, and grow spiritually, a church where you can find happiness and fulfillment.

SIMPLY SPEAKING

The New Testament does not envisage solitary religion; some kind of regular assembly for worship and instruction is everywhere taken for granted in the Epistles. So we must be regular practicing members of the church.

C. S. LEWIS

☺ LIVING THE HAPPY LIFE

Are you currently involved in a church family of your own? If not, make the commitment to begin looking for a body of believers in which you can participate.

APPRECIATE WHAT YOU HAVE.

*Better one handful with tranquility than two handfuls with toil and
chasing after the wind.*

ECCLESIASTES 4:6

When it comes to what you have—and don't have—
gratitude is largely a choice. It all boils down to where you fix
your focus. Instead of being envious of others, feeling discontent
and unhappy, you can choose to be thankful.

Spend a few minutes each morning reflecting on the
blessings God has given you. No matter what shape your home is
in, begin to thank God for a secure shelter, a place to stay warm
and dry. If you don't have a reliable car, thank Him for bringing
the bus route so close to your house. Thank Him for the basics:
food on the table, a bed to sleep in, clothes to wear, a way to earn
a living.

Thank Him also for those blessings that are not material
in nature, such as health, a sound mind, the love of family and
friends. Finally, remember that if you belong to God through
faith in Jesus, you have also received God's greatest, most
important blessings: His constant presence with you on earth
and the promise of eternity with Him in heaven.

Many people watch their lives slip through their fingers

while they whine about all they're missing. They acknowledge
only the negatives. Focusing on the positives has two effects:
it allows you to be grateful for what you have while boosting
your faith to believe that with God's help things will get better.
Gratitude comes from knowing God is on your side and will
provide everything you really need.

SIMPLY SPEAKING

*Contentment is understanding that if I am
not satisfied with what I have, I will never be
satisfied with what I want.*

BILL GOTHARD

☺ LIVING THE HAPPY LIFE

*L*ist ten things you are thankful for. Why not write God a letter
sharing your appreciation?

NEVER COMPROMISE THE TRUTH.

The truth will set you free.

JOHN 8:32

Truth is a precious, glorious thing. Never sell it short—it is a rock on which you can build a fulfilling, happy life. That's because every little aspect of truth, even the smallest glimmer of it, is a reflection of the ultimate, joyful truth that God exists and that all His great and wonderful promises are real. It must be guarded with jealous zeal, protected at all costs.

You may be saying to yourself, *Actually, I've never had a problem with honesty.* That may be true—and then again, maybe it isn't completely true.

Have you ever embellished the facts to make a point or get a laugh? Do you sometimes engage in flattery in order to manipulate another person? Do you live behind a mask, projecting a false image, because you fear you won't be liked for who you really are?

Few people lie under oath or con others with bold-faced lies. Most just let go of the truth a little here and a little there. It's said that the captain of a ship crossing the ocean must keep his vessel unswervingly on course. One degree in any direction can cause him to miss his port completely.

Guaranteed, simple honesty is hard work. But it's worth it. When you respect yourself, others will respect you as well. Always strive to be completely honest with God, with others, and with yourself. This will allow you to swing the door of your heart wide open. Then you'll discover that happiness has been sitting there on the doorstep all along.

SIMPLY SPEAKING 📣

The man who speaks the truth is always at ease.

PERSIAN PROVERB

☺ **LIVING THE HAPPY LIFE**

Honesty is always the best policy.
Begin to live a life of truth today.

DON'T TRY TO CHANGE OTHERS.

Accept one another, then, just as Christ accepted you.

ROMANS 15:7

Once you realize that it's not your job to change people, and that you can't do it anyway, you'll start breathing a lot easier. You'll discover that your life is suddenly more peaceful—with more room for happiness.

It's easy for even the best, most benevolent people to get caught up in this happiness-destroyer because it seems to seek the well-being of others. What wife hasn't thought her husband would be a much better person if only he were more _____? Husbands often have the same thought: *If my wife would wear her hair longer or wear more makeup, she'd be so much prettier.*

Parents also fall into this trap. Lovingly and with the best intentions, they often try to mold their children into the people they want them to be—for their own good, of course. Even coworkers and friends can be the objects of our charitable makeover strategies.

The truth of the matter is that the only One who can change another person is God. The Creator knows when change is needed and He has his ways of bringing it about. Certainly He expects us to hold each other accountable in regard to dangerous or destructive behaviors. But when it comes to the core of who a person is, that job rests with God.

Try appreciating the good in other people. Celebrate their strong points, the positive aspects of their character and personalities. When it comes to the not-so-good part, be patient, relax, and leave the changing to God. This leaves you free to relate to and enjoy the people in your life, and that is sure to bring far more happiness into your world.

SIMPLY SPEAKING
Do not be angry that you cannot make others
as you would wish them to be, since you cannot
make yourself as you wish to be.

THOMAS À KEMPIS

☺ LIVING THE HAPPY LIFE

Think of one person you would really like to change. Now think
of five positive attributes you know he or she already has. Why
not share your positive thoughts with that person? You just
might make his or her day!

LAUGH AT YOURSELF.

Be joyful always.

1 THESSALONIANS 5:16

Raising your happiness quotient may be possible without changing the circumstances of your life at all. Maybe all you need to change is the way you look at your life. Perspective is everything, you know!

Perhaps you have been viewing your life as a drama, filled with emotional tension and a sober sense of the challenges you are facing. Try, instead, to see your life as a comedy.

Think for a moment about the last movie you saw with a comedic twist. Certain things are true of any movie you choose. The protagonist faces a veritable mountain of obstacles and adverse circumstances, right? But you laugh at them because you can appreciate the irony—the twisted humor—when the main character locks his keys in the car and tries to snatch them from the ignition by dangling his belt through the sunroof. Remember the movie *National Lampoon's Vacation*? The family leaves on a trip across country to visit a theme park and they encounter every possible misfortune on the way. It's hilarious!

Another thing about comedies is that they always have a happy ending. What if you had the solid assurance that your story was going to end beautifully as well? What peace of mind you would have! How liberated you would be to laugh at your own failures and inadequacies! That's the wonderful thing about placing your life in God's hands. You can be certain that you will have the happiest of all endings.

Become the director of a whole new movie, and let the laughs begin!

SIMPLY SPEAKING 📢

The ability to laugh at life is right at the top . . . in the hierarchy of our needs. Humor has much to do with pain; it exaggerates the anxieties and absurdities we feel, so that we gain distance and through laughter, relief.

SARA DAVIDSON

☺ LIVING THE HAPPY LIFE

When was the last time you had a good belly laugh? Why not find something humorous about your life today and laugh out loud?

SPEND TIME WITH THE WISE.

He who walks with the wise grows wise.

PROVERBS 13:20

Have you ever searched for your glasses only to find that they are sitting on top of your head? What about your car keys? Have you ever frantically looked under couch cushions and on countertops, even in the refrigerator, only to find them in your pants pocket or purse? Sometimes what you're looking for is right under your nose, you just can't see it. The secrets of happiness are like that sometimes.

In every life, there is someone—a teacher, a parent, a grandparent, a friend, a coworker, a pastor, a neighbor—who exhibits wisdom. And wise people know a lot of secrets! Often, though, we dismiss the familiar and search frantically for more exotic sources of enlightenment. How silly when what we need has been in plain sight all along.

Look around you for these valuable people in your life. Once you see them for who they are, move in with your questions. You will almost certainly discover that they are eager to give you the answers they've found—lessons learned the hard way through hardship and suffering. Uncle Ernie might tell you that he received seventy-two rejection letters before experiencing the happiness of seeing his first novel in print. Secret #1: Happiness is sometimes deferred. Grandma Huber may share with you that she's learned to look for those little crystalline moments of happiness in each day rather than waiting for some grand event in the future. Secret #2: True happiness is around us all the time if we're looking.

Make some time for the wise people in your life. Open your heart to ask questions and then listen to what they have to say. Your answers about happiness may be hiding in plain sight.

SIMPLY SPEAKING 📢
The next best thing to being wise oneself is to live in a circle of those who are.

C. S. LEWIS

☺ **LIVING THE HAPPY LIFE**

Who are the wise people in your life? Be sure to make time for them—their influence is priceless.

RESPECT BOUNDARIES.

Do not move your neighbor's boundary stone.

DEUTERONOMY 19:14

It's said that good fences make good neighbors. This
principle extends to friends and family members as well.
Everyone has personal boundaries, and just as you respect the
lines between your property and your neighbors', it's a good idea
to honor people's personal boundaries. Doing so shows regard
for the people God loves. It will also help establish harmony in
your relationships, promoting an atmosphere of joy in all your
interactions with others.

There are many kinds of personal boundaries. They apply to
things like the amount of time people are willing to give, the level
of emotional intimacy they will permit, what type of activities
they want to participate in, what commitments they are willing
to make, what possessions they want to share. For example, if the
parents of your children's friends have set restrictions on the TV
programs their kids watch, you would do well to enforce those
limits while their children are in your home. If your friend isn't
comfortable sharing details of a certain situation, you should
treat that respectfully.

Good communication is the key to understanding other

people's personal boundaries. When you sense that certain
territory may be off-limits, invite others to show you where their
boundaries lie. This will demonstrate that you care about their
feelings. Most people will be happy to point out to you the lines
they don't want crossed. Your relationship will immediately be
strengthened, thanks to the mutual respect that such a conversation fosters.

Anything you can do to show others that you understand
where you leave off and they begin will enhance your relationships, making it easier for you and the people in your life to enjoy
a peaceful, happy coexistence.

SIMPLY SPEAKING

*Boundaries help us define what is not on our
property and what we are not responsible for. We
are not, for example, responsible for other people.
Nowhere are we commanded to have "other-
control," although we spend a lot of time and
energy trying to get it!*

DR. HENRY CLOUD AND DR. JOHN TOWNSEND

☺ LIVING THE HAPPY LIFE

What kinds of boundaries have you set with the people in your
life? Are they healthy or unhealthy? What can you do to establish
happy, healthy interactions with the ones you love?

LOVE WITH RECKLESS ABANDON.

Follow the way of love.

1 CORINTHIANS 14:1

Imagine for a moment how God loves: freely, passionately, wholeheartedly. His love is generous and unrestrained. Even though there's always a chance His love will be rejected, He never withholds it. He goes on loving regardless of the risk—one might say almost recklessly. God has given you the ability to love as He loves, with the same abandon, and therein lies one of the primary keys to happiness.

Since human love is in reality selfish, it tends to hold back, protecting the tender ego inside. Instinctively it gravitates toward the safety of those who are sure to receive and return the gift offered. But the soul infused with God's love can love anytime, anyplace, anyone.

The great woman of faith Corrie ten Boom survived the horrors of the Holocaust, losing her family and spending years in a Nazi concentration camp. Many years later she came face-to-face with one of the camp's cruelest tormentors. She could have spat in his face, thrashed him verbally—who would have blamed her? Instead, she extended her hand and let the love of God flow through her. She dared to love with reckless abandon.

You may never be in such a situation, face-to-face with someone you have cause to hate, but you will certainly have opportunities to love the unlovely, the disenfranchised, the lonely, the obnoxious, the careless, the undeserving. You can choose to love with reckless abandon as well. Except that in God's hands, your recklessness becomes His opportunity to reshape human hearts. And your reward: a degree of happiness you have never known before.

SIMPLY SPEAKING 📢

I have found the paradox that if I love until it hurts, then there is no hurt, but only more love.

MOTHER TERESA

☺ LIVING THE HAPPY LIFE

Whom do you need to love with "reckless abandon"? Why not begin to let God love that person through you today?

DEVELOP SELF-DISCIPLINE.

*God did not give us a spirit of cowardice, but rather a spirit of power
and of love and of self-discipline.*

2 TIMOTHY 1:7 NRSV

A graceful dance, a moving instrumental performance, an
inspiring vocal solo: each brings incredible satisfaction and
joy to both artist and audience. Yet none are possible without
self-discipline. Creative expression offers human beings an
experience of freedom and exhilaration, but that can be achieved
only through hours of study and practice.

This is true in so many areas of life. Do you want to be able
to fly? You'll have to invest a lot of time and effort in ground
school, learning all about aerodynamics, the controls and instru-
ments of an airplane, navigation, weather, radio communication,
and the many rules of aviation. You'll also have to spend time in
the air with an instructor, developing and practicing the skills
needed to pilot an aircraft. It's only through such diligence that
you'll ever know the thrill and adventure of flying solo.

Discipline is a key to making good grades at school, honing
athletic ability, advancing in a career, staying healthy, managing
finances. It's also the key to growing spiritually—that is,
deepening your relationship with God and becoming more like

Him. That's important because there's no greater happiness to be found in life than in an intimate connection with God. In fact, all the other wonderful experiences that life offers will ultimately feel empty if He isn't in the picture. A living, growing relationship with God will enrich every aspect of your life.

Make an effort to learn about spiritual disciplines such as Bible study, meditation, prayer, and fasting. Then begin to put them into practice. God has provided these disciplines for your benefit, knowing they will help you draw closer to Him. Spiritual discipline will take you into God's presence, where you'll discover a joy that can be found nowhere else.

SIMPLY SPEAKING

No one is free who is not a master of himself.

EPICTETUS

☺ LIVING THE HAPPY LIFE

Spiritual discipline isn't always fun or easy—but it will lead to a happy life!

DREAM BIG!

When I was woven together in the depths of the earth,
your eyes saw my unformed body. All the days ordained for me
were written in your book.

PSALM 139:15–16

God is the Maker and Master of the farthest reaches of the universe, of the infinitely large and the infinitely small. He rules over the vastness of time—past, present, and future. His goals involve all of humanity and all eternity. Is there any question that His plans for you will be greater than your most elaborate dreams for yourself?

God made you with particular talents and abilities, interests, and passions. He has molded you through your upbringing, your education, and your experience. And He has placed you on this earth at a very specific point in time. His purpose for you fits perfectly into the awesome, wonderful story He is writing, allowing you to have an impact upon the lives of generations of people.

If you've always imagined that the dream in your heart is nothing more than a product of your wild imagination or a feeble attempt to achieve self-worth, you could well be selling yourself and God terribly short. Ask Him to clarify the passion you feel inside and fill you with a sense of excitement and enthusiasm if He is indeed the initiator of the dream you carry inside. Not only will He confirm your destiny, He will lead you every step of the way as you pursue and fulfill His perfect plan for you.

Your dream may be small right now—constricted by the limitations of your own mind and experience, but as you happily place your hand in God's hand, you will see your dream expanding. Like the moon emerging from behind the clouds, revealing more and more of its milky splendor, your dream will emerge revealing more and more of God's amazing purpose. Get ready to dream big!

SIMPLY SPEAKING

No dreamer is ever too small;
no dream is ever too big.

AUTHOR UNKNOWN

☺ LIVING THE HAPPY LIFE

What dream has God placed in your heart that has yet to be fulfilled? Don't give up—God wants you to dream big so that He can help you bring those dreams to pass.

REFUSE TO BE A VICTIM.

We are more than conquerors through him who loved us.

ROMANS 8:37

Life sometimes places us in adverse circumstances, and we often have to deal with situations we cannot control. This is true for kings and paupers alike. Ecclesiastes 9:11 says, "The race is not to the swift or the battle to the strong, nor does food come to the wise or wealth to the brilliant or favor to the learned; but time and chance happen to them all." We cannot always successfully avoid tragedy and suffering, but we can control how we respond to it.

Many people never bounce back after a traumatic situation occurs in their lives. They choose not to. Soon the helplessness they felt invades every corner of their hearts and minds, effectively keeping them from enjoying the happiness still on the docket for their lives.

You can't choose for others—but you can choose for yourself. That may mean deciding to put a certain event out of your mind so you can move on or seeking out the help you need to properly recover. Either way, God is waiting to take your hand and help you find the path around the obstacle that has stopped you in your tracks.

No matter what you've faced in the past, you can feel happiness again. You can live and laugh and enjoy your life. God promises: "When you pass through the waters, I will be with you; and when you pass through the rivers, they will not sweep over you. / When you walk through the fire, you will not be burned" (Isa. 43:2). Take Him at His Word and begin to identify again with the joy of being alive.

SIMPLY SPEAKING

Suffering would be altogether intolerable—if there were no God.

F. J. SHEED

☺ LIVING THE HAPPY LIFE

Are you living under the shadow of a past event? Why not pour your heart out to God, asking Him to take your hand and help you release this burden and go on with your life?

SHARE YOUR GOOD THOUGHTS.

Encourage one another daily.

HEBREWS 3:13

So many times we have good thoughts about people and for one reason or another, we keep them to ourselves—right where they will never do any good for anyone. They won't cheer a discouraged heart, bolster someone's self-esteem, strengthen the bonds of friendship, provide a moment of happiness for us or for anyone else. To accomplish those things, we must transform thoughts into spoken words.

Words are powerful, and we are often reminded to watch what we say because our words can do harm. If that's true, the opposite must be true as well: good words can help others. The Bible says it this way, "When you talk, do not say harmful things, but say what people need—words that will help others become stronger" (Eph. 4:29 NCV).

Your happiness will be magnified when you make an intentional effort to communicate to others the good thoughts and feelings you have toward them. As you do, keep in mind that an uplifting tone of voice and a bright, heartwarming smile go hand in hand with edifying words. The sincerity in your voice and the approval on your face will go miles in expressing the love in your heart.

Go ahead and tell your sister that you love her recipe for lasagna and no one makes it better. Let your daughter know you like the way her eyebrows dance when she's enjoying herself. Tell your neighbor his yard looks nice and the man at the vegetable market the produce is really fresh. Do more than think it, say it! It's a happiness-grabber all around.

SIMPLY SPEAKING 📢

Kind words can be short and easy to speak, but their echoes are truly endless.

MOTHER TERESA

☺ **LIVING THE HAPPY LIFE**

What good thoughts do you need to share with your loved ones today? Don't wait another minute—your happiness, and theirs, depends on it!

LIVE FOR TODAY.

This is the day the LORD has made; let us rejoice and be glad in it.

PSALM 118:24

Yesterday is but a memory and tomorrow doesn't yet exist. We are so used to projecting both forward and back that we tend to miss this important fact. All the life we really have is rolled up in this day, this moment in time.

When your mind has acclimated to this truth, you'll see that your happiness quotient is transformed. No longer must you look back longingly at a happier time or forward to some ambiguous point in the future. You realize that you can be happy—right now. What a revelation!

Practice living in the present by making yourself consciously aware of where you are and what you're doing moment to moment. This will feel a lot like work at times. Your busy mind will want to anticipate what comes next—it's been trained that way. Have you ever driven across town and couldn't remember getting there? That's a common experience. Your body was in the car, but your brain was focused on what comes next.

Try this simple exercise. Focus your mind on your surroundings, the ticking of the clock, the sound of the wind in the trees, even the beating of your own heart. Take deep breaths and thank God for every bit of beauty around you. As you practice "now thinking," your mind will begin to put things in proper perspective.

It isn't that the past and the future are of no value to you. Certainly you should learn from the past and prepare for the future. The problem comes when one or both become the primary focus of your attention, robbing you of the reality of the present. Now is a terrible thing to waste!

SIMPLY SPEAKING

We have only this moment, sparkling like a star in our hand . . . and melting like a snowflake. Let us use it before it is too late.

MARIE BEYNON RAY

☺ LIVING THE HAPPY LIFE

Determine to put the past behind you and to not worry about the future. How will you live for today, today?

TAKE A DEEP BREATH!

The LORD God formed the man from the dust of the ground and
breathed into his nostrils the breath of life.

GENESIS 2:7

Many people wouldn't think of missing their vitamin supplements or energy drinks for even a day. What these conscientious individuals may not realize is that as much as 75 percent of the energy in their bodies is provided by the oxygen taken in by the simple act of breathing—when it's done properly.

Deep breathing—pulling air well into the abdominal area, filling and emptying the lungs with each inhalation and exhalation—has enormous health benefits. It can:

1. Reduce stress by keeping it from building up in the body.
2. Relax muscles, relieving back, neck, and stomach pain.
3. Strengthen the immune system, releasing a mighty army to fight bacteria, viruses, allergens, parasites, infections, and other dangerous invaders.
4. Prevent premature aging by invigorating skin cells.
5. Assist digestion.
6. Boost energy levels.
7. Stabilize emotions and general well-being.

It's difficult to imagine that something so available, so

natural, so easy to do can make such a difference in your life, your health, and your happiness quotient. Best of all it's free and can be practiced literally anywhere. All those supplements and energy drinks won't hurt you, but they can't come close to providing the benefits God placed in one single breath.

Determine to make breathing a priority. Breathe in and breathe out, deeply, effectively—and thank God for the privilege each time you do.

SIMPLY SPEAKING

Youth will never live to age unless they keep themselves in breath with exercise, and in heart with joyfulness.

SIR P. SIDNEY

☺ LIVING THE HAPPY LIFE

Close your eyes and inhale deeply. Now exhale, allowing all of your problems and worries to drift away in that one single breath.

ADD A LITTLE CULTURE TO YOUR LIFE.

Lift your eyes and look to the heavens: Who created all these?
He who brings out the starry host one by one,
and calls them each by name.

ISAIAH 40:26

Creative expression is one of God's greatest gifts to humankind, evidence that His creative nature is reflected in people everywhere. Whether we're looking up at the exquisite beauty of the night sky or listening to an incredible banjo solo, the arts give us an opportunity to experience deep inner happiness.

The range of the arts is so vast as to be almost limitless:

1. The visual arts include but are not limited to painting, sculpture, film, photography, crafts, architecture, design, and fashion.

2. The performing arts include but are not limited to theater, dance, musicals, circuses, opera, and music.

3. The language arts include poetry, fiction, essays, plays, and other forms of creative writing.

4. The culinary arts include baking, cake decorating, and every imaginable form of creative cooking and food preparation.

Are you surprised? You may have thought that appreciating the arts meant sitting through some high-brow affair while dressed in a penguin suit or evening gown. In reality there is something special, inspirational, and truly moving for every individual taste and pocketbook.

You may be wowed by the artistry of a graceful figure skater or moved to tears by the reading of an extraordinary piece of literature. It doesn't matter what you choose as long as you indulge yourself in the goodness of it all. Drink it in until you feel the happiness bubbling up inside.

SIMPLY SPEAKING

Culture is a little like dropping an Alka-Seltzer into a glass—you don't see it, but somehow it does something.

HANS ENZENSBERGER

☺ LIVING THE HAPPY LIFE

What cultural event can you attend in the next week? In the next month? Determine to set a date—and allow yourself to experience the artistry and passion of the culture around you.

SIT BY THE BED OF A DYING CHRISTIAN.

O death, where is thy sting? O grave, where is thy victory?

1 CORINTHIANS 15:55 KJV

Since you're searching for happiness, it's likely that you have in your mind a certain concept of what happiness is. You should know that the mental image you have may be more a stereotype than a reality. For example, have you ever seen a smile on the face of someone who is suffering? People who can smile through pain have found a level of happiness that bypasses their present circumstances and grounds itself deep in God. If you're looking for something deeper than superficial, temporary happiness, you'll have to leave the sunlit mountaintops and venture into the valley below.

Go to the proving grounds, the places where people who have invested their faith and hope in God's promises discover that the happiness He gives them is tough and lasting. Spend time with Christians who are experiencing hardship and pain. Visit believers who are struggling with illness. Go to godly men and women who are approaching the ends of their lives, and sit for a while beside their beds. You'll likely see happiness within them radiating through the darkness, and it will well up in your own heart as well.

Their happiness comes from an inner knowing based in both revelation and experience. They see that this life is little more than a vapor, a fleeting moment in the course of eternity. Their focus is not on the suffering, the dying, the struggling. It isn't on the circumstance they are going through at that particular moment. Their eyes are looking beyond the crisis to the glory on the other side. The Bible says: "Let us fix our eyes on Jesus, the author and perfecter of our faith, who for the joy set before him endured the cross, scorning its shame, and sat down at the right hand of the throne of God" (Heb. 12:2).

You can have that kind of deep, abiding happiness. Look for it in the valleys of your life.

SIMPLY SPEAKING

The final heartbeat for the Christian is not the mysterious conclusion to a meaningless existence. It is, rather, the grand beginning to a life that will never end.

JAMES DOBSON

☺ LIVING THE HAPPY LIFE

$\mathcal{L}$ook for God in the mountaintops—and in the valleys—of life. You can have His happiness no matter what circumstances you find yourself in.

REALIZE THE SOURCE OF TRUE HAPPINESS.

Choose for yourselves this day whom you will serve.

JOSHUA 24:15

God created you, gave you life, and placed you here on earth. That's pretty incredible in and of itself—but there's more! God has also given you a free will. You choose for yourself the path to happiness. And that's exactly what people do. One chooses the path of acquiring wealth, another, fame. Others seek sensual pleasures and selfish indulgences. Happy for a moment—then poof! Happiness is gone. Still others seek power, and some try to impress God with their works.

Their Creator grieves to see them wasting their time running after false gods and momentary pleasures. He knows they will be deeply disappointed in the end. But He does not interfere. Instead, He stands by and gently encourages them to turn away from those empty pursuits and be reconciled to Him. He promises that when they do, they will know happiness as they have never known it before.

Perhaps you have been seeking the key to happiness. You wonder why you just can't find the formula. It could be that you've been looking for happiness in all the wrong places. You have yet to make the one choice that will get you what you so desperately want and need. Choose happiness by choosing God. Once you know Him, you will wonder how you ever lived before, what motivated you, how you dealt with the pain and heartache. You will wonder how you missed what was there all the time. Why did it take so long to hear His voice saying "Choose Me. Choose Me"?

SIMPLY SPEAKING 📢

God gave us a free choice because there is no significance to love that knows no alternative.

JAMES C. DOBSON

🙂 LIVING THE HAPPY LIFE

Have you chosen God and given Him first place in your heart? If not, why not invite Him into your life today? You will begin to experience true happiness as you've never known before.

LEARN THE CIVILIZED ART OF CONVERSATION.

Let your conversation be always full of grace.

COLOSSIANS 4:6

Conversation is a lost art—and it's no wonder. Who has time to sit around and talk when there are schedules to keep, games to play, television and movies to watch, work to do? You know how it is. Of course, we stay in touch with those we love, but it comes in bits and snatches: a minute or two as you pass each other in the morning, and a couple of minutes on the cell phone during the day.

In earlier times, before technology made it possible for us to lead runaway lives, people spent happy hours each and every day just talking. They conversed in the garden, in the parlor, around the dinner table, in front of the fireplace, on the front porch, over the back fence—anywhere they found themselves. They took time to speak to shopkeepers and friends they passed on the street. Verbal interaction was more than an exchange of information; it was a pastime, an activity that brought them great enjoyment—yes, even happiness.

We can't go back to those good old days. But we can find ways to transport the joys of conversation into our busy lifestyles.

It will take some doing, of course. But here are some suggestions to get you started:

- Eat your evening meal at the table at least twice a week.
- Plan a party once a month. Invite your guests to sit around and talk by placing chairs in small groupings.
- First thing in the morning or the last thing at night, set aside thirty minutes just to talk with your spouse. Avoid sensitive subjects. Talk instead about your hopes and dreams.

Once you get started, you'll find lots of things to talk about and lots of happiness as well.

SIMPLY SPEAKING

Inject a few raisins of conversation into the tasteless dough of existence.

O. HENRY

☺ **LIVING THE HAPPY LIFE**

How can you make the lost art of conversation a part of your daily life? Make the commitment today to talk to your friends and loved ones more—who knows what all they have to say?

GO AHEAD AND CHANGE THINGS UP.

[Jesus said,] I tell you the truth, unless you change and become like little children, you will never enter the kingdom of heaven.

MATTHEW 18:3

Remember how exciting it was, when you were a child, to do something different like sleep upside down, with your head at the foot of the bed? Kids get a big kick out of little novelties. They love to spread out sleeping bags on the living room floor or set up a tent in the backyard. Without having to make big plans or go anywhere or spend a bunch of money, they find joy simply by bursting free from their everyday routine and trying something new.

Why should children have all the fun? You can add more happiness to your life by keeping it fresh and interesting. Mix things up now and then. It'll keep you from falling into a rut—or help pull you out of the one you're in. Spend a night on the foldaway couch in the den, or treat yourself to an overnighter in your own guest room. A little change once in a while is stimulating and rejuvenating.

Incorporate variety into your way of living. Adopt a pattern of trying new patterns occasionally. Keep your lifestyle and your attitude dust-free! Breaking old paradigms will increase your opportunities for happiness. It will also allow you to experience God in new ways, shattering the box you try to keep Him in, changing your entire perception of His goodness, power, and majesty.

When you sleep upside down, you see your bedroom from a whole new perspective. And when you sleep out under the stars, you see the universe the same way. God can use your openness, your willingness to look at everything with fresh eyes, to teach you wonderful truths about who He is. Life's little changes invite simple pleasures—and keep your senses alert to the many ways God can speak to you.

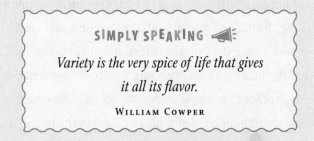

SIMPLY SPEAKING

*Variety is the very spice of life that gives
it all its flavor.*

WILLIAM COWPER

☺ LIVING THE HAPPY LIFE

Why not take a new approach to prayer? Instead of praying in your usual place, take a prayer walk. Not only will you enjoy God's beautiful creation, but you will also experience a new vitality in your quiet time with Him.

DON'T EXPECT GRATITUDE.

Your Father, who sees what is done in secret, will reward you.

MATTHEW 6:4

Do you find pleasure in helping others, giving of your time, money, talents, and resources? If so, you're in for a lifetime of happy moments—provided you don't sabotage yourself by placing your happiness in someone else's hands.

That's what you're doing when you expect gratitude from those you reach out to help. Of course, it's nice when you get it, but what happens when you don't? Too often such disappointment causes feelings of resentment, disharmony, and anger. These emotions are happiness-busters! It's much better to give from the heart with no expectation of reward—verbal or otherwise—other than the satisfaction you feel knowing you have done something good and pleased God in the process.

Of course, people should say "Thank you," but too often they don't. Sometimes they forget to and other times they simply take your kindness for granted. Most often they're just distracted and preoccupied. Maybe they'll come back someday and say those magic words, and maybe they won't. It's better not to hang your happiness on that fence post. God has created us to be givers just as He is. Because of that, doing for others has its own reward—happiness and personal satisfaction.

Next time your neighbor asks you to water her plants while she's away on vacation or your coworker could use some help preparing for a big presentation—wherever you see fit to lend a helping hand—do it for the right reason: because you feel good about it.

Your life is in your hands and so is your happiness. Guard it carefully, seeing that your expectations are in the deed itself rather than in the flawed nature of humankind. You'll be glad you did.

SIMPLY SPEAKING

An effort made for the happiness of others lifts
above ourselves.

L. M. CHILD

☺ LIVING THE HAPPY LIFE

Whom do you need to thank today? Express your appreciation to those around you and watch their happiness grow.

NEVER SKIMP ON SAYING "I LOVE YOU."

[Jesus said,] A new command I give you: Love one another.

JOHN 13:34

How often do you tell your family and friends that you love them? Some people wait their whole lives to hear those words— and never do. What a tragedy. You can't change what others do, but you can be sure that doesn't happen to the people you love.

This doesn't have to be a forced thing. The best way is to say it when you feel it, every time you feel it. That could be when you're tying your six-year-old's shoe or helping your grandmother into her bed. You might feel love suddenly wash over you while you're sitting next to your spouse at a baseball game. It doesn't matter really. Thoughts of love come often to us. Just let the words follow.

You certainly shouldn't worry about overusing that remark-able phrase, "I love you." People never seem to tire of hearing it. Even if they blush or look away or stand before you speechless, they like it, you can be sure of that. Of course, there may be some situations when your words might be inappropriate. Remember that you mean to bless rather than embarrass.

When you confirm your love often, it helps to banish

insecurity, loneliness, fear, worthlessness, and a host of other happiness-busters. Those around you will be happier and that means you will too. You can't make others happy without getting a little on you.

It is true that actions speak louder than words, and actions without words lose a great deal of their power. Make sure your loved ones have an abundance of both.

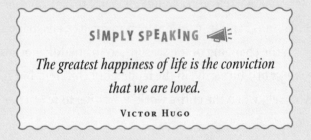

SIMPLY SPEAKING

The greatest happiness of life is the conviction that we are loved.

VICTOR HUGO

☺ LIVING THE HAPPY LIFE

*L*ove is an amazing force. The more you give it away, the more it comes back to you! To whom will you give it away today?

LEAVE HOME.

The whole earth is full of his glory.

ISAIAH 6:3

You don't have to travel anywhere to witness God's glory reflected in a sunrise or sunset, to see it exhibited in a sky filled with clouds or stars. You could live all your life on a one-acre parcel of ground and be continually reminded of His magnificence—in the changing of the seasons, in the budding of a tree, in the wings of a butterfly, in the laughter of children. But why limit yourself, when the entire world is waiting to reveal God's splendor?

Stand upon Maine's rocky shoreline as the sun sends its first dazzling sparkles across the Atlantic. Drive along the coast of California as the sun touches the Pacific, igniting the western sky. Watch clouds soar over the hills of Montana, and marvel at the stars as you stroll along a Florida beach at night. The world is God's creation, it's yours to delight in, and if you take every chance to experience its incredible beauty, your heart will overflow with praise, gratitude, and happiness.

Everywhere you go on this planet, you'll witness God's glory. You'll see it in the beauty of the earth, the grandeur of the ocean, the elegance of a river or lake, the loveliness of the sky. As you travel, however, pay closest attention to the faces of the people you meet. That's where you'll behold the greatest display of God's craftsmanship. And as you listen to His children tell stories of how He has provided for them and protected them and guided them and blessed them, you'll glimpse an aspect of God's glory that will thrill you more than everything else—His loving heart.

SIMPLY SPEAKING

The world is a great book, of which they who never stir from home read only a page.

THOMAS C. HALIBURTON

🙂 LIVING THE HAPPY LIFE

Where do you plan to take your next trip?
Be sure to include some time to enjoy the beauty of God's creation—wherever you go.

TAKE OFF YOUR SHOES.

*[Jesus] said to them, "Come with me by yourselves to a quiet place
and get some rest."*

MARK 6:31

You derive great joy from fulfilling God's purposes for you.
Doing the various kinds of work He has given you to do—in your
office, church, home, or elsewhere—brings you a lot of satisfaction. You love God and the people He cares about, and you'd
serve Him around the clock if you could. But God knows you
can't keep at it 24/7. It wouldn't be healthy for your mind, body,
or spirit. God designed you to sleep for a significant portion of
each day, and He set aside one day a week for you to rest and
recuperate. In light of all that, He surely won't mind if you take a
little time each day to kick off your shoes and relax.

A break like that is just what you need to get reenergized
for the rest of the day. It's also the perfect opportunity to spend
some quality time with God. A quick time-out during a hectic
day will refresh more than just your body if you use a few of
those minutes to pray. Find a nice, quiet spot someplace where
you can get comfortable, forget the cares of the day for a while,
and connect with God. Don't worry about being barefoot as you
talk with Him—remember, when Moses met God for the first

time, God insisted that he take off his sandals!

Jesus once invited His disciples to escape from all the hustle and bustle around them and join Him for some peace and solitude. Even if you're at work, shut the door for a few minutes, kick off your shoes, and take a few deep, relaxing breaths. Your workdays will be much happier.

SIMPLY SPEAKING

There is no music in a rest, but there is the
making of music in it.

JOHN RUSKIN

☺ LIVING THE HAPPY LIFE

When was the last time you ran barefoot through a thick patch of grass? What better way to relax than by kicking off your shoes and letting your feet sink into God's wonderful green carpet?

HONOR YOUR FATHER AND MOTHER.

"Honour your father and mother"—this is the first commandment
with a promise: "so that it may be well with you and you may
live long on the earth."

EPHESIANS 6:2–3 NRSV

Being a parent is definitely not an easy job! God has given
parents a monumental task—not only are they to protect, guide,
and lovingly discipline the children God has entrusted to them,
but they eventually have to release them into this crazy world so
that they can find their own destinies. Parenting requires many
selfless acts and many prayers and tears along the way. And it is
very sobering to know that God will one day hold every parent
responsible for this task.

Sometimes we as children forget just how daunting this is,
and we may criticize our parents or hold grudges against them
for past failures. All of us make mistakes, so it is important to
note that most parents truly desire to be good parents. They
want to do what is best for their children. They choose to
sacrifice their own interests and needs many times for the sake of
their children, and they do it willingly.

If you are blessed to have such parents, you are blessed
indeed. And if your parents didn't display these characteristics,

it is possible that they did the best they could under the circum-stances. If not, God can still heal the wounds in your heart so that you can give them respect for His sake.

At any age, our parents are worthy of our honor and respect. Even if their efforts are less than perfect, we owe them that much. God not only suggests it; He commands it. He even adds a promise to it—happiness in the form of a long and prosperous life.

SIMPLY SPEAKING

We never know the love of a parent until we become parents ourselves.

HENRY WARD BEECHER

☺ LIVING THE HAPPY LIFE

*I*n what way can you actively honor and respect your parents today? Maybe a phone call, a card, or even a visit would express your appreciation for all that they have done for you.

DEVELOP GOOD HABITS.

The fear of the LORD *is the beginning of wisdom;*
all those who practise it have a good understanding.

PSALM 111:10 NRSV

Researchers believe that after twenty-one days of repetition
an action becomes a habit. Some believe it takes even less time.
Whatever the case, establishing good habits will set the stage
for a happier, more fulfilling life. These habits in particular will
stoke up your happiness quotient:

- Read your Bible and pray daily.
- Put things back where you found them.
- Hold your tongue when you're angry.
- See your doctor regularly.
- Brush your teeth after every meal.
- Be punctual.
- Lock your car.
- Exercise.
- Attend church regularly.
- Wash your hands before you eat.
- Always say "Thank you."
- Close the door behind you.
- Keep a checkbook register.

- Drive the speed limit.
- Call your parents once a week.

Of course, there are many other good habits that can make your life easier and help you avoid pain and hardship. But those listed here will help you get started as you make proactive changes to better your life. Start now and in three short weeks, you'll have mastered your most unruly opponent—yourself.

SIMPLY SPEAKING

Any act often repeated soon forms a habit; and habit allowed, steadily gains in strength.

TRYON EDWARDS

☺ LIVING THE HAPPY LIFE

Think of one good habit you would like to begin. Now set your plan—and make it happen!

DON'T GO NEAR THE G-WORD
—GOSSIP.

A perverse man stirs up dissension,
and a gossip separates close friends.

PROVERBS 16:28

Ever played the Gossip game? Everyone sits in a circle. One
person starts the game by whispering something in the ear of the
person next to him. That person in turn whispers what he heard
or thinks he heard into the ear of the person on the other side of
him. And so on around the circle. The last person in the circle
then repeats aloud what was whispered into his ear. Most of the
time, it isn't even close to what the first person said. This game is
called Gossip because it is a reasonable facsimile of what happens
in reality.

In the childhood game of Gossip, no one gets hurt. It's all in
fun. But the real life consequences of listening to and repeating
unsubstantiated rumors can be devastating to your happiness
and the happiness of others. It's a mystery why our human
natures want to grab and spread unflattering information,
why we seem to relish it, even take pleasure in it. But the Bible
assures us that with God's help we can overrule our fallen human
tendencies in favor of His perfect ways of love.

Resolve never to engage in gossip. When it comes your way, choose to "just say no." Like alcohol and drugs, it's dangerous and destructive. It will be challenging for a time, especially until people get the message that you're not interested in hearing what they have to say. You may feel some hostility when you take a stand. A few may justify their actions by putting you down. Underneath, though, they know you're right. And you will probably feel as if you're out of the loop, at least for a while. Soon, though, you'll be able to see that your high-road strategy is paying off in peace of mind and an ability to look others in the eye.

SIMPLY SPEAKING

A wound caused by words is more painful than a wound caused by an arrow.

ARABIAN PROVERB

☺ LIVING THE HAPPY LIFE

What will you do the next time a friend comes to you with a juicy tidbit of information? Make the determination today to take the high road and not let gossip be a part of your life.

PRACTICE THE GOLDEN RULE.

In everything do to others as you would have them do to you;
for this is the law and the prophets.

MATTHEW 7:12 NRSV

If you want others to treat you well, do the same for them.
Put into practice what you would like to see happen in your own
life. That's the Golden Rule in a nutshell. Ask yourself how you
would want to be treated in particular circumstances, such as the
following:

- Someone finds your purse on the side of the road with
  money and identification inside.

- You need to change lanes in rush-hour traffic.

- You're on crutches from a skiing accident and need
  assistance with your grocery bags.

- At the supermarket checkout, you come up a quarter
  short.

- You accidentally step on someone's toe.

- Your small child is separated from you in a department
  store.

- Your dog gets out of the yard and eats your neighbor's
  flower bed.

- Your husband is late getting home from work.

- You're involved in a fender bender.
- Your neighbor's mail shows up in your box.

Now turn the circumstances around. You're on the giving end this time. If you put the Golden Rule into practice, you're going to return the purse and money you find on the side of the road, you'll be willing to hang back and let another driver change lanes in front of you during rush-hour traffic, and so on down the list.

The Golden Rule doesn't apply only to certain people or certain situations. It applies to everyone—family as well as friends, even strangers. Everyone will not reciprocate in like manner, but for those who do, you'll be happy and grateful.

SIMPLY SPEAKING

We have committed the Golden Rule to memory;
let us now commit it to life.

EDWIN MARKHAM

☺ LIVING THE HAPPY LIFE

Jesus said to "do unto others as you would have them do unto you." When was the last time you put the Golden Rule into practice? How could you put it into practice this week?

STAY OUT OF OTHER PEOPLE'S BUSINESS.

Let us stop passing judgment on one another.

ROMANS 14:13

You mean well—certainly that's true. You sense that if you could just get through to your friend or your child or your spouse, everyone would be happier. You could really help, save that person some heartache, some disappointment, some adverse circumstance. But oddly enough, you receive a negative response for your trouble. Sound familiar?

You aren't alone. Most everyone has indulged the temptation to offer unsolicited advice, to meddle. It's one thing to be aware, tuned in, available to your family and friends, but inserting yourself and your opinions into personal matters can bear unpleasant results, such as broken relationships, delayed maturity, enabling of destructive behaviors, resentment, and interference with God's plan and purpose.

The indirect result of interfering in the affairs of others is that you unnecessarily increase your stress level and burden yourself with problems that are out of your control. It's not a position that promotes happiness and general well-being. The Bible says that we are to give our heavy burdens to the Lord. He certainly doesn't ask us to do that so that we can load up on the burdens of others.

Unless you see a situation where someone is physically or emotionally at risk, make it a habit to squelch nosiness and curiosity when it comes to the affairs of others. If you find yourself tempted, close your eyes and picture yourself stepping out of the way and letting God step in. Whisper a prayer for those involved and remind yourself that God is big enough to handle their situation. If He needs your help, He'll let you know. Walking away will feel bad for a short time, but soon you will feel your happiness quotient rising.

> SIMPLY SPEAKING ◀€
> *Knowing that I'm not the one in control gives*
> *great encouragement. Knowing the One who is in*
> *control is everything.*
> ALEXANDER MICHAEL

☺ LIVING THE HAPPY LIFE

What is a situation in a friend's or loved one's life that you need to walk away from? How can you continue to be supportive from a healthy distance?

JUST *BE* HAPPY.

As [a man] thinketh in his heart, so is he.

PROVERBS 23:7 KJV

Just be happy. Sounds too simplistic, doesn't it? But, in actuality, we can have much more happiness if we choose to consider things from a positive perspective. Everyone experiences the ups and downs of life. However, we can make a decision to dwell on the negative or practice what the old saying says to do: When life give you lemons, make lemonade! It really boils down to your attitude, and you have the ability to mold your attitude into any shape you like. Here are some tips:

- Ignore those who tell you that life is too difficult to be happy. What do they know?
- When you awaken each morning, be thankful for another day, even if it's raining. (Read 1 Thessalonians 5:18.)
- Smile at those you meet even if they don't return the favor.
- Don't borrow trouble. Each day has enough of its own. (Read Matthew 6:34.)
- Don't allow trouble to bury you in its gray mire of sorrow.

- Don't give in to negative thinking. (Read 1 Thessalonians 5:16.)
- Be positive even when others are not. Refuse to give up on anything worth having or doing.
- Do something you enjoy each day, even if it's just a walk in your neighborhood.
- Whistle as you go through the day. (Read Psalm 95:1.)
- Work at being happy because it's worth it.

You're human like everyone else, and from time to time you need a little pick-me-up in your decision to be happy. When you reach that stage, find someone else who has decided to be happy. Join forces with him or her and march forward in your decision to be a happy person. (Read Psalm 146:5.)

SIMPLY SPEAKING 📢

A happy person is not a person in a certain set of circumstances, but rather a person with a certain set of attitudes.

HUGH DOWNS

☺ LIVING THE HAPPY LIFE

*C*hoose today to *just be happy*—as much as it depends on you!

SCHEDULE YOUR HAPPINESS.

I will greatly rejoice in the LORD,
My soul shall be joyful in my God.

ISAIAH 61:10 NKJV

For the majority of people in this world, work is drudgery.
They labor at it because they have no choice, and it produces
no joy or satisfaction. It is simply what they must do to survive.
Precious few are privileged to be able to work full-time at a job
they feel passionately about. It would be easy for the rest to
simply become resigned to a certain level of unhappiness—but it
doesn't have to be that way.

If your work doesn't touch upon your gifts and talents
and you aren't in a position to change that, you can still
schedule those things into other parts of your life. You may
love to cook but find yourself working at a stuffy office
job—unfulfilled and unhappy. Try inviting some of your
coworkers for dinner one night and giving expression to
your love of cooking. They will probably be thrilled to come.
Perhaps you have artistic talent but your job has you selling
real estate. You feel your creativity becoming more stifled day
after exhausting day. Though many people would love to do
what you do, it brings you no real happiness. Signing up for

an evening art course may be all that is needed to reset your happiness meter and give you a new lease on life.

God has placed gifts and talents in each of us. His intention was not to frustrate us but to lift our self-worth and give us a lust for life. You may be one of the fortunate ones who gets to exercise your talent every day through your work. But if that isn't the case, schedule those things into your life and you'll feel your inner happiness begin to glow.

SIMPLY SPEAKING

If you have a talent, use it in every which way possible.

JOHANN VON SCHILLER

☺ LIVING THE HAPPY LIFE

Why not pencil in some time for happiness? Open your daily planner, pick a time, and then mark it in. Don't let anything interfere with that appointment—and be sure to do something fun with your special time!

LEARN SOMETHING NEW.

[God] put a new song in my mouth, a hymn of praise to our God.

PSALM 40:3

Happy people are interesting people because they are always exploring new territory. "New territory" doesn't have to mean an undertaking that will require piles of money or a large amount of time or extraordinary intellectual output. You don't have to learn to speak Chinese or become a concert pianist. But you could learn a new vocabulary word this week or master a new cooking technique. You could pick up a magazine in a waiting room and read about something new that strikes your interest—something like:

- How to lay a brick patio.
- How to play chess.
- How to grow African violets.
- How to create a Web site.

You could also:

- Volunteer to work in a soup kitchen and learn how to work in that environment with energy and grace.
- Ask your grandmother to teach you how to make perfect gravy or the right way to iron a shirt.
- Take a tour of a museum or a factory and discover how

little you know about steel or blown glass.

- Spend an evening learning how to activate the hidden features on your cell phone.
- Find a new way to praise and worship God.

Seize the opportunities that come your way. If somebody offers you free scuba diving lessons, what have you got to lose by giving it a try? There are whole worlds of knowledge out there waiting to be explored. Your key word is *new*. Decide to learn something new today.

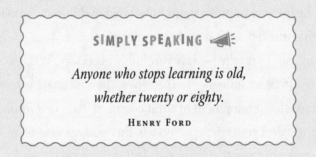

SIMPLY SPEAKING

Anyone who stops learning is old,
whether twenty or eighty.

HENRY FORD

☺ LIVING THE HAPPY LIFE

What one new thing can you learn this week? This month? This year? Never lose your curiosity or thirst for knowledge!

LET YOUR CHILDREN GROW UP.

May your father and mother be glad;
may she who gave you birth rejoice!

PROVERBS 23:25

Part of the job of parenting—arguably the hardest part—is letting your children grow up. It feels like separating your limbs from your body in some ways. That's natural. God has given you a strong instinct to protect and care for your children. Growing past that instinct as God leads is a tall order.

Difficult as it may be, it is absolutely necessary. While you will always be an influence in their lives, their ultimate survival demands the development of adult coping skills. Their future happiness and yours depends on whether you are able to let your children learn from their mistakes and make good choices.

Consider these tips:

- Allow your children, even when they are small, to make some choices for themselves—for example, those that reflect personal style and taste.
- As they grow, encourage your children to express their own opinions—even when they differ from yours.
- Allow your children to learn prudence by suffering the consequences of their actions.

- Resist the urge to do for your children what they can do for themselves.
- Encourage your children to develop faith and dependence on God.
- Expect your children to act responsibly.
- When your children are adults, treat them like adults.

Parenting is a blessing, a privilege, and an awesome responsibility. You put your all into it. But don't worry, as your children grow up and leave home, your happiness won't float out the door behind them. Sure, you might shed a few tears as they drive away, but knowing you've equipped them for happy lives will make yours happy as well.

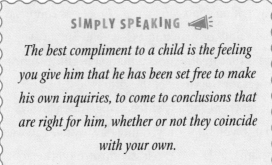

SIMPLY SPEAKING

The best compliment to a child is the feeling you give him that he has been set free to make his own inquiries, to come to conclusions that are right for him, whether or not they coincide with your own.

ALISTAIR COOKE

☺ LIVING THE HAPPY LIFE

What skills do your children need to learn in order to grow into capable, functioning adults? How can you begin to teach those skills as early as possible?

RESPECT THE ENVIRONMENT.

Have dominion over the fish of the sea and over the birds of the air
and over every living thing that moves upon the earth.

GENESIS 1:28 NRSV

Clear blue skies, sparkling, clean water, white sandy beaches, a rich abundance of wildlife, birds, fish, and other natural resources: these are just a few of the pleasures God has placed here on Earth for us. In fact, the earth is one of the most spectacular, extravagant, luxuriant gifts ever given. And happily we are the recipients—God Almighty the Giver!

Clearly, taking good care of our planet has countless benefits for each of us and for mankind as a whole. But an even greater motivation is that treating this remarkable gift with respect shows respect for the Giver of the gift.

If your mother carefully stitched together a lovely quilt and presented it to you on your wedding day, would you want her to visit your home and see it carelessly thrown on the floor? What about the macaroni necklace your granddaughter made for you at school? Gifts represent the people who gave them. And this earth represents the God who created it for us.

Taking care of the planet is too big a job for any one or ten or ten thousand of us to manage, but we can all do our part to make this a place where we can live happy, blessing-filled lives. Here are some suggestions you may want to consider:

- Don't litter.
- Observe ozone alert days.
- Conserve valuable natural resources: water, trees, etc.
- Carpool or use public transportation when possible.
- Recycle: bottles, aluminum cans, plastic, newspapers.
- Properly dispose of any polluting waste in your care: batteries, oil and gas products, paint, chemicals, etc.
- Put your groceries in paper bags rather than plastic.
- Take it easy with lawn chemicals.
- Teach your children to leave their space on the planet better than they found it.

SIMPLY SPEAKING 📢

We have forgotten how to be good guests, how to walk lightly on the earth as other creatures do.

AUTHOR UNKNOWN

😊 LIVING THE HAPPY LIFE

Make the commitment today to respect the environment, the planet God has entrusted to us. Why not write up a plan—the specific things you intend to do—and place it in a prominent place in your household, say, on your refrigerator? That way, everyone will remember—and participate!

GET HOOKED ON SIMPLE ACTS OF KINDNESS.

Always try to be kind to each other and to everyone else.

1 THESSALONIANS 5:15

It's absolutely true that the best way to be happy is to make others happy. If you're skeptical, try including a few simple acts of kindness in your day, and see for yourself.

Somehow in our society, we have come to believe that happiness is attained by getting all we can for ourselves. This is the opposite of what the Bible teaches. The lesson there is that happiness is gained by giving. You may not be able to give billions like Bill Gates and Warren Buffet, but that doesn't matter. The principle works the same for both great gifts and small.

People all around you need to hear kind words of encouragement, see a friendly smile, receive a warm hug or pat on the back. In a single day, you will find hundreds of opportunities to bestow simple kindnesses—if you're looking for them.

You should be warned, however: many have found the practice of kindness highly addictive. The happiness and satisfaction they feel makes them yearn for more. One day they're showing simple kindness to their coworkers, neighbors, family, friends, and the occasional stranger, and before they know it, they find themselves visiting nursing homes, orphanages, shelters, participating in community services, eager to help wherever they can make a difference. For those, there is no going back to the days of selfishness and insensitivity to others. They're hooked!

Open your heart, expand your borders, and practice kindness. When you do, the happiness in your life will rise with each passing day.

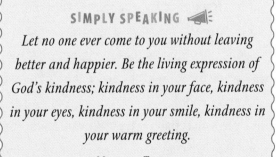

SIMPLY SPEAKING

Let no one ever come to you without leaving better and happier. Be the living expression of God's kindness; kindness in your face, kindness in your eyes, kindness in your smile, kindness in your warm greeting.

MOTHER TERESA

☺ LIVING THE HAPPY LIFE

When was the last time you spontaneously extended kindness to someone?

CARE ABOUT THOSE THINGS GOD CARES ABOUT.

The world and its desire are passing away,
but those who do the will of God live for ever.

1 JOHN 2:17 NRSV

Look on your calendar, read through your daily planner, check out your Blackberry and you'll find out what you care about—your interests, your favorite things, your most loved pursuits. Now ask yourself: *how much does God care about those things?* It's a good question and the answer can surprise you, hopefully cause you to look a little harder at how you set your priorities and order your life.

The principle here is that we typically care about the things that touch our lives each day. God cares about those things too. But He also cares about much more. God cares about the suffering of people around the globe. He cares about their earthly lives and their eternal souls. He cares about the injustices of war and godliness of nations. He cares about birth and death and how we live in between. God cares about you.

God cares about you in a different way than you care about yourself, however. He cares that you are in vital relationship with Him through His Son Jesus. He cares that you are living in such a way that you are an example to those whose lives you touch. He cares that your life makes a difference for eternity.

God doesn't expect you to toss your Blackberry or cancel all activities in your planner. He just wants you to attain to more, to care about the issues that shake the earth and produce eternal consequences. The next time you find yourself in prayer, before you ask Him to help you with the things you care about—ask Him what you can do to help with the things He cares about. You'll soon find that you're happy to feel the beat of His heart.

SIMPLY SPEAKING

Live near to God, and so all things will appear to you little in comparison with eternal realities.

ROBERT M'CHEYNE

☺ **LIVING THE HAPPY LIFE**

In your prayer time, begin to consider your priorities. Are they the same as God's? If not, how can some of them begin to change?

SEE AGE AS AN ACCOMPLISHMENT RATHER THAN A CURSE.

Gray hair is a crown of splendor; it is attained by a righteous life.

PROVERBS 16:31

Don't confuse the pursuit of happiness with a quest for the fountain of youth. Life is a one-way street, and the best way to live it is to embrace the delights the journey offers, joyfully anticipating the bliss you'll experience when you reach your destination. If you're following Jesus, you're walking on the road that leads to paradise. So being "over the hill" is a wonderful thing—you're halfway to heaven.

You have every reason to feel good about the stage of life you're in, even as you pass through middle age and step into the senior years. Spiritually, you're just hitting your stride. With your cooperation, God has been developing your character for a long time. Although He will continue molding you for the rest of your life, stop and consider what the two of you have accomplished!

All the right choices you have made, God has honored. They may have been difficult to make at the time and may even have resulted in short-term hardship, but ultimately they have brought you blessings. Each time you've done things God's way,

He has rewarded you with joy, with a closer relationship with Him, and with more inner strength to go on choosing well.

As for your poor choices (we have all made some), God has proven His awesome power to take what's wrong and use it for right. He has given you wisdom and maturity through your mistakes and used their consequences as another way to shape your character—and amazingly, to guide your steps and bring you to the very place He wants you to be at this point in your journey.

Wear your age well as you travel onward, sharing with other travelers the benefits of your experience, thankful for all God has done, and happily looking forward to everything He will do.

SIMPLY SPEAKING

To be happy, we must be true to nature, and carry our age along with us.

WILLIAM HAZLITT

☺ LIVING THE HAPPY LIFE

For your next birthday, plan a party to celebrate!

GIVE YOURSELF A BREAK.

[Jesus said,] Come to me, all you who are weary and burdened,
and I will give you rest.

MATTHEW 11:28

Experts say that the oldest child typically ends up juggling a
mountain of responsibility for others—even as an adult. These
chronic overachievers grow up looking after their siblings and
serving as Mom and Dad's right hand. By the time they're grown,
they have acquired a deep sense that their self-worth comes from
being good (so as not to add additional stress to Mom and Dad),
they feel responsible for the actions of others ("I thought I told
you to watch him!"), and they micromanage situations in an
effort to keep the road ahead smooth for everyone.

If this sounds like the story of your life, you should know there
is not one drop of happiness in that package. It will keep you and
your true potential completely subdued, held down by issues of
perfectionism and control, both exercises in failure and frustration.

But you can be free from these tendencies before they take
a toll on your relationships, your health, and your self-esteem.
Begin by honestly looking for these warning signs:

- The tendency to be too involved with the details of your
  adult children's lives.

- The tendency to try to control others, especially your spouse—"for their own good."
- An inability to rejoice in your achievements.
- Unrealistic expectations of yourself and others.

You deserve to be free to follow your own path to happiness, to know that God loves you not for what you do but for who you are—His own unique creation.

It won't be easy, but it's in your power to give yourself a break. Begin by asking a trusted friend or family member to help you pinpoint your improper responses to specific situations as they come up. Simple enlightenment goes a long way. But if you find you aren't making progress on your own, seek help from a counselor—your happiness is hanging in the balance.

SIMPLY SPEAKING

Forget about doing everything right; you'll never get there. Forget about keeping everyone safe; you don't have the power. Forget about playing God. He's one of a kind.

ANDREA GARNEY

☺ LIVING THE HAPPY LIFE

*H*ow might you begin to "let go and let God" rule in your daily life?

BE EXTRAVAGANTLY GENEROUS.

[Jesus said,] Give, and it will be given to you. A good measure, pressed
down, shaken together and running over, will be poured into your lap.
For with the measure you use, it will be measured to you.

LUKE 6:38

If you want your money to go farther, give it away. Oddly
enough, money brings you more happiness when you place it in
someone else's hand. And the joy it puts in your heart remains.

Have you ever spent a lot of money on yourself and then
tried to hold on to the joy it gives? Say you've recently gone all
out to remodel a room in your house: new paint, new flooring,
new curtains, new furniture. It was exciting and satisfying when
the room was finished and you stood there looking around
admiringly. Days later you went out of your way to peek into the
room to recapture that feeling. But before long, those little visits
weren't quite so thrilling, and eventually you stopped taking
detours at all. The room was nice, but no big deal anymore.

Contrast that experience with the time your friends, who had
always struggled financially, needed a car, and you decided to
give them one of yours. Every time you see them in that car, God
reminds you of the look on their faces when you handed them
the keys. The joy you felt that day still burns brightly.

Both of these situations brought happiness to your life, but the second one was shared and multiplied. It's the reward of giving.

God loves extravagant givers because He is an extravagant Giver. He derives great pleasure from blessing His children. When you give extravagantly to your church, to charitable organizations, and to people in need around you, you're reflecting God's character, and He will reward you with the same deep, enduring joy that fills His generous heart. There's no better use for your money, no investment anywhere that produces such a wonderful return.

SIMPLY SPEAKING 📢

You do not have to be rich to be generous. If he has the spirit of true generosity, a pauper can give like a prince.

CORRINE U. WELLS

☺ LIVING THE HAPPY LIFE

Whom can you bless extravagantly today? The more generously you give, the more blessings will be poured out on your own life.

RID YOUR HEART OF EVERY TRACE OF PREJUDICE.

Man looks at the outward appearance, but the LORD looks at the heart.

1 SAMUEL 16:7

Prejudice is an insidious happiness-buster. Not only does it weaken and hinder our human relationships, it intrudes on our relationships with God. By failing to accept and value others, we are in essence failing to accept and value Him.

You may think you don't have any prejudices. Most of us think that. But prejudice is funny that way. It often disguises itself as other things. Have you ever said something like: "I'm sorry, that's just the way they are." This is prejudice disguised as truth. Prejudice can also come disguised as fact: "They just can't be trusted." It even comes dressed as kindness and caring: "Marrying outside your race just causes problems for your children." Of course, these statements are not truthful, factual, or kind and caring. They are excuses for refusing to accept every person as a unique human soul created in God's own image.

Getting rid of deep-seated prejudicial attitudes involves some heavy lifting. It's like removing old appliances; you can't do it alone. And God, like anybody who comes into another person's house to help with a cleanup project, won't haul away anything you haven't given Him permission to get rid of. You have to choose to send your wrong attitudes out the door.

But what a trade-off! Once the job is done, you'll stop judging others by their outward appearance and start taking the time to discover who they really are. You'll be open to relationships with a more diverse group of people—many of whom you'll grow to love. Your heart, now rid of fear and distrust, will have ample room for acceptance and joy.

SIMPLY SPEAKING

Prejudice is the child of ignorance.

WILLIAM HAZLITT

☺ **LIVING THE HAPPY LIFE**

What subtle prejudices have crept into your attitudes, actions, and statements? Why not ask God today to help you purge yourself of these prejudices? You'll live a happier life as a result.

DON'T LET ANGER CAPSIZE YOUR SHIP.

In your anger do not sin.

EPHESIANS 4:26

When anger flares, it's like a sudden storm at sea. You're sailing along peacefully and happily, on course and in control, when suddenly you find yourself caught up in a tempest. If you're wise, you'll steer into the wind while it lasts, holding steady, resisting the urge to lash out. That way you'll weather the storm with minimal damage, and when it's over, you can quickly get back on course and up to speed.

Like storms at sea—a necessary climatic event—anger often gets a bad rap. In its purest state, it's simply an element of human nature, and it does provide wind for our sails by motivating us to stand up to injustice, sin, and evil of all kinds— even in ourselves. Without it, we would be unable to properly respond to the world around us. Even Jesus showed His anger when He overturned the tables of the merchants who were doing business within the walls of the temple. Anger is a bad thing only when we allow it to overwhelm us, control us, and cause us to wrongfully lash out at others. This happens when our anger is based on ego rather than ethics.

You are the captain of your ship. You decide how you will respond to angry feelings when they come your way. Increased happiness calls for keeping your hands firmly on the wheel, regardless of how you are provoked, and listening to God's voice inside rather than the music of self: "He hurt my feelings." "She never does what I tell her to do." "He's pushing my buttons." "Those kids won't give me a moment's peace."

Take that critical moment to identify the root of the anger you are feeling and deal with it accordingly. With God's help, you can harness the anger in your life and make it work for you rather than against you.

SIMPLY SPEAKING

A person is as big as the things that make him angry.

WINSTON CHURCHILL

☺ LIVING THE HAPPY LIFE

The next time a storm of anger threatens to capsize your ship, determine to maintain control. Count to ten, remain calm, and assess the situation—and don't forget to ask God for His help.

FIND A MENTOR—BE A MENTOR.

Follow my example, as I follow the example of Christ.

1 CORINTHIANS 11:1

It's one thing to learn principles about living happily. It's another thing to have someone older and wiser than you show you how you can apply these truths to everyday life. A mentor, someone who has lived long enough to know where the rubber meets the road, can demonstrate practical ways of doing what it takes to live joyfully. So you may want to consider finding someone who can serve as your own personal mentor.

It's not hard to identify the people who would make good mentors. They're the ones striving earnestly to live the kind of life that pleases God. They're also the ones with a sense of joy about them, because they're already reaping the rewards God promises to everyone who learns the principles of right living and implements them in their lives. Once you've found someone you think would make a good mentor, pray about your choice. God can tip you off if the person isn't all he or she seems to be. Then simply take the initiative and ask. If that person cannot take the time, don't give up. Pray that God will send you just the right person.

When you do find that special person, here are a few

suggestions to help you glean the most from the relationship: Meet together on a regular basis. Make the time a priority. Be humble and willing to learn. Ask lots of questions. Show your gratitude to this person for being willing to invest in your life.

As you follow in the footsteps of a godly mentor, you'll soon discover that you've picked up some street smarts of your own, wisdom from which a younger person could benefit. You may even want to consider becoming a mentor yourself!

SIMPLY SPEAKING

Learn from the mistakes of others. You can't live long enough to make them all yourself.

AUTHOR UNKNOWN

☺ LIVING THE HAPPY LIFE

If you have never been mentored, ask the Lord to send someone into your life from whom you can learn. If you are a seasoned believer, you may want to volunteer to mentor someone else.

BE YOURSELF.

I praise you because I am fearfully and wonderfully made;
your works are wonderful, I know that full well.

PSALM 139:14

If it's true that each snowflake, every leaf that falls from a tree, is unique, why would anyone imagine that human beings—God's greatest and most beloved creation—are all alike? And yet, conformity is the rule rather than the exception. Your inner happiness depends on your ability to see and celebrate who you really are—the one-of-a-kind person God created.

There are many reasons why people don't often feel comfortable with who they are inside:

- Societal standards. These are actually a good thing. They show us where the boundaries of civilized behavior begin and end. However, they become a negative influence when they are applied as a strict code rather than loose guidelines: "Girls should be quiet and demure, while guys should be blunt and assertive."

- Parental expectations. The Bible tells us to honor our fathers and mothers, and we should all do that without allowing it to swallow up our own sense of who we are: "Of course you'll be a teacher, just as we were."

- Limited perspective of others. People have opinions about who you are based on who you are to them: "Women don't make good race-car drivers." "Men don't stay home with their children." It's easy to let that slide—easier than digging down deep and finding out who you are to you.

God loves you deeply, both for the qualities you have today and for the immense potential He has poured into you. Ask Him to help you identify those characteristics that define who you truly are. Then as God gives you insight, begin to celebrate as the real you comes shining through.

SIMPLY SPEAKING

Be who you are and say what you feel because those who mind don't matter and those who matter don't mind.

DR. SEUSS

☺ LIVING THE HAPPY LIFE

List five qualities that make you uniquely you. Thank God for making you one of a kind!

STAY ON THE HIGHWAY TO HEAVEN.

*You have made known to me the path of life; you will fill me with joy
in your presence, with eternal pleasures at your right hand.*

PSALM 16:11

In your pursuit of happiness, check out every lead, gather
all the advice you can, draw from the experience of others, learn
from every available source, but remember this above all else:
unless your life is headed, day after day, week after week, month
after month, toward heaven and perfect communion with God,
your happiness will not last. In fact, it will flare up for a time and
then disappear. It cannot—will not—be sustainable.

Complete and perfect happiness can be found only in
God's presence, at that time when the circuit of redemption,
repentance, reconciliation, and renewal is completed in the
kingdom of heaven. Our lives here on earth cannot enter that
completeness, but as we travel toward the goal, happiness tags
along as our faithful companion.

If you have ever done something wrong, something
you are sure has hurt your heavenly Father, you know that
once you repent, say you're sorry, determine to get back on
the right path, an incredible sense of happiness follows. It
sweeps over us not because we've failed, but because we got

back on our feet and back on the path God has for our lives.

Don't be fooled. True, enduring happiness is not a result of money, fame, possessions, status, or prestige. All those things are temporary. They might bring you fleeting happiness in this life, but they won't do a thing for you in the life to come. The happiness that comes from knowing God, however—that lasts forever, and ever, and ever, and ever.

SIMPLY SPEAKING 📢

Complete happiness is knowing God.

JOHN CALVIN

☺ LIVING THE HAPPY LIFE

In your busy life, it may be easy to forget to spend quality time with your heavenly Father. Why not get away to a quiet place and reconnect with God in a fresh way today?

STRIVE TO BE A WORLD-CHANGER.

Be steadfast, immovable, always excelling in the work of the Lord,
because you know that in the Lord your labour is not in vain.

1 CORINTHIANS 15:58 NRSV

Think about all the bigger-than-life figures you've read about who have made a big difference in the world at large: Alexander Graham Bell with his invention of the telephone. Mother Teresa with her care of India's outcasts. Bill Gates with his millions of dollars in charitable donations. You may think you can't come close to making these kinds of contributions to the world you live in—but you might be wrong.

It's pretty certain that these great contributors and others did not set out to change the world; it just happened as they were doing what they did. Bell was just working hard on an idea, Mother Teresa simply caring for society's helpless, and Gates following his dream. They just kept going, each day doing what came naturally to the best of their abilities—and greatness followed.

God calls all of us to be world-changers. He asks us to do each day what we can to make things better, brighter, more comfortable, more loving for those around us. He asks that we develop our gifts, use the resources He's provided for us, and be faithful day to day. When we do, He promises to multiply the work of our hands and make our ordinary contributions extraordinary (see Psalm 90:17).

The happiest, most satisfied people in the world are those who are doing all they can where God has planted them. They aren't worried about the big picture. They have discovered that the road to greatness is paved in everyday possibilities and actions. Ask God what you should be doing to make your mark on Planet Earth.

SIMPLY SPEAKING 📣

The difference between what we do and what we are capable of doing would suffice to solve most of the world's problems.

MAHATMA GANDHI

☺ LIVING THE HAPPY LIFE

What are the things you know God has called you to do on a day-to-day basis? How might your daily consistency and obedience to God eventually change the world?

LIVE VICARIOUSLY—THROUGH BOOKS.

Whatever was written in former days was written for our instruction,
so that by steadfastness and by the encouragement of the scriptures
we might have hope.

ROMANS 15:4 NRSV

The exploits found between the pages of a new volume can leave you breathless with excitement. It doesn't matter what year the book was published. Any book is new if you're reading it for the first time. And like some vacation trips, stories can be so enjoyable, you may want to go a second time—reopening the door to a familiar place, experiencing the happiness of old literary friends.

From the time you learned to read, your world changed. You made friends with the characters in your books. Revisit the pages of your favorite stories and renew old acquaintances. Or pick up a never-before-read volume and meet new friends. You can laugh and cry along with people you've never met and feel a certain kinship with them as you enter their worlds. You can share their experiences without ever leaving the comfort of your home.

Not everyone prefers the same kind of book. Some like history, others prefer romance, while another gets lost in a suspense novel. One book that offers something for everyone is the Bible. Open the pages of this timeless tome and you'll find romance between Ruth and Boaz, suspense in the story of David and King Saul, friendship between Jonathan and David. It's a readers' feast.

Stretch yourself by reading in areas you've never tried before. Ask other readers for a list of their favorite books. Discover *The New York Times Book Review* and online book reviews.

You may not be able to travel around the world, but you can take a vicarious journey through the characters in your books. Say good-bye to boredom, hello to happiness.

SIMPLY SPEAKING 📣

Everywhere I have sought rest and not found it, except sitting in a corner by myself with a little book.

THOMAS À KEMPIS

🙂 LIVING THE HAPPY LIFE

*W*hich are your all-time favorite books? Why did you choose these particular titles? Make the decision to read at least one of these "old friends" sometime in the near future.

BE ON THE LOOKOUT FOR EVERYDAY MIRACLES.

You are the God who performs miracles;
you display your power among the peoples.

PSALM 77:14

Miracles are everywhere—if you're looking: A baby is found
alive in a trash can. A man survives a plane crash. A woman
is pinned in her car underneath a semi on the interstate, but
she comes out without a scratch. A boy's leukemia goes into
remission. A girl is struck by lightning, a thousand volts surge
through her body, but she doesn't have even one burn.

Miracles—God's handiwork—are all around us. They are
in the train that slowed down and prevented an accident five
miles up the road, and the baby whose parents never expected
to have children. They are especially present in the most difficult
situations in life: The soldier whose life was spared because he
turned to walk away just before a bomb exploded. The job that
came along just as a family reached the end of its savings.

There are also the miracles that come with a smile when
you're feeling isolated and alone, the encouraging word when
you're feeling discouraged and defeated, the sunshiny day when
you're feeling dark and gloomy inside.

Everyday miracles are an everyday reality, and a giant boost to your happiness quotient. Ask God to open your eyes to His handiwork around you each day. Ask Him to help you see and feel the wonders of His love and grace. Once you've grown accustomed to recognizing the everyday miracles, your faith will be strengthened and your trust in God renewed. You'll find yourself under the spout where the glory comes out, living a life of supernatural provision, protection, and blessing.

SIMPLY SPEAKING

It is not necessary for me to go far afield in search of miracles. I am a miracle myself. My physical birth and my soul's existence are miracles. First and foremost, the fact that I was even born is a miracle.

TOYOHIKO KAGAWA

😊 LIVING THE HAPPY LIFE

Name one "everyday miracle" you have experienced recently. Why not write a prayer thanking God for the miracles He brings into your life?

NEVER GIVE UP!

Let us not become weary in doing good, for at the proper time we will reap a harvest if we do not give up.

GALATIANS 6:9

A robin makes her nest. But as she goes to get more twigs, when she returns, she finds another bird has destroyed her work, but she is undeterred—she starts over. No matter how many times her efforts are thwarted by animals, elements, or circumstances outside her control, the robin's resolve never falters. She's determined to do what she has been created to do.

God wants us to have the same determination the robin has—to never give up on the dreams He has placed in our hearts. He knows a lot of things are going to challenge us—we may lose our direction, be victimized by others, and have to start over many times—but He wants us to stick with it for as long as it takes, never giving up.

What adversities are you facing as you go about the life God has called you to? Maybe your bills are far more than your weekly income. Maybe your marriage is on the rocks and there's no resolution in sight. Maybe you're stuck in a nothing job but can't find anything else. Are you sick of trying and not getting any farther ahead? Are you ready to just give up? Maybe you already have.

God is bigger than any of your problems. He created you to be a winner—not a quitter. So even if you've thrown in the towel, it's never too late. You can take a deep breath and start over one more time. And as you do, you can know beyond a shadow of a doubt that He is there to help you, encourage you, and strengthen you (just as He does that little robin) until the task is finished.

SIMPLY SPEAKING

Most of the important things in the world have been accomplished by people who have kept on trying when there seemed to be no hope at all.

DALE CARNEGIE

☺ LIVING THE HAPPY LIFE

When was the last time you persevered through a difficult situation? How did God bring you through?

BUY A GOOD BED.

He grants sleep to those he loves.

PSALM 127:2

You spend about a third of your life sleeping. If you sleep for eight hours each night, you rack up fifty-six hours a week in dreamland—2,912 hours a year. By age seventy, you'll have slumbered for 203,840 hours. That's twenty-three years' worth of sleep!

One way to make your days more joyful is to make your nights more comfortable. Buy yourself the best bed you can afford. That way you'll be well rested each morning and won't have to suffer as many aches and pains, so you'll be in a much better mood throughout the day. Get a bed with a spring system designed to support your body adequately and evenly, and with a good cushion on top to give the bed a soft feel.

Then, since you're taking steps to ensure yourself a great night's sleep, purchase a high-quality pillow too! Anything you can do to help yourself sleep more soundly will make you feel more refreshed and invigorated every morning, and that will certainly add happiness to your life.

There are other things you can do to fall asleep more easily and stay asleep all night. Avoid caffeine, especially in the latter part of the day. Turn off the TV earlier in the evening, since intense programs may keep you awake when you're ready to go to bed. Drink some warm milk before bedtime. And develop the habit of meditating on God's promises as you lie in bed and drift off to sleep. That's the best way to calm your mind and keep from lying awake worrying half the night. You might also try reflecting on God's blessings and thanking Him for all of them—including the nice, cozy bed you have.

SIMPLY SPEAKING

O bed! O bed! Delicious bed! That heaven upon earth to the weary head.

THOMAS HOOD

☺ LIVING THE HAPPY LIFE

What are five blessings on which you can meditate tonight as you drift to sleep?

GROW YOUR OWN BOUQUET.

See! The winter is past; the rains are over and gone.
Flowers appear on the earth; the season of singing has come.

SONG OF SONGS 2:11–12

Daffodils, morning glories, day lilies, irises, roses—many
varieties, many blooms, each the essence of happiness on a stem.
Surround yourself with them and you might feel you've created
a new world. And you don't need to go far to find or create this
kind of beauty. You can grow many varieties you may never
see at the local florist: cosmos, phlox, sunflowers, zinnias, and
bishop's lace, or the common species such as roses, daisies, and
chrysanthemums. Here are some suggestions to help you get
started:

- Pick a garden spot. Choose a sunny site protected
  from the wind. Clean out all weeds. Loosen the soil
  with a spade. Add compost or other organic material
  to improve your soil. When the danger of frost is past,
  you're ready to plant.

- Decide what you'd like to grow and how many of each
  plant you need.

- Use either seeds or seedlings according to package
  instructions. Keep soil moist until seedlings emerge.

Thin plants as directed on seed packets.

- Water as needed and weed often.
- The more you cut, the more blooms your plants will produce, so indulge your fancy with the beautiful blossoms you've grown. Fill vases for several rooms of your house. Share these bouquets of color with those close to you. Indulge your love of giving to others by filling their homes with the same floral extravagance you enjoy.

Being able to breathe in God's creative beauty is a wonderful way to start your day and give your happiness quotient a shot in the arm.

SIMPLY SPEAKING

The Earth laughs in flowers.

RALPH WALDO EMERSON

☺ LIVING THE HAPPY LIFE

List three of your favorite flowers. Why are they your favorites? Take some time to remind God of how grateful you are for His beautiful creation.

READ YOUR BIBLE EVERY DAY.

All Scripture is God-breathed and is useful for teaching, rebuking,
correcting and training in righteousness, so that the man of God may
be thoroughly equipped for every good work.

2 TIMOTHY 3:16–17

Reading feeds the mind as well as the soul, and you can't do
better than a daily dose of wisdom and guidance from the Bible.
It offers something special for every circumstance, attitude, and
doubt.

If you're in need of wisdom, you should head straight for the
book of Proverbs. Given by God, these sayings convey timeless
wisdom that has resonated throughout the centuries. David's
psalms are a wonderful source of comfort and solace—just what
you need if you desire to praise God in the midst of your trials.
It's also an opportunity to read arguably the most beautiful
poetry ever written.

Do you wonder about the timeless battle being played
out in the Middle East? Trace the history of Abraham and his
descendants from Genesis to Malachi. Walk in the footsteps
of Jesus as you read the Gospels, listening to Jesus' words and
reading the disciples' eyewitness accounts of His miracles. As
you read through the New Testament, you'll be able to ride

along with the apostle Paul on his missionary journeys.

Choose a quiet, restful time of the day for your Bible reading: perhaps early in the morning before the activities of the day are scheduled to begin or before you climb into bed each night— guaranteed to sweeten your dreams.

If you would like to organize your reading, there are many good reading schedules to choose from. You can find them online and at your local Christian bookstore.

You can't overestimate the short- and long-term benefits of reading the Bible—even if it's just a small portion—each day. All the happiness worth having resides within its pages.

SIMPLY SPEAKING

I have found in the Bible words for my inmost thoughts, songs for my joy, utterances for my hidden griefs and pleadings for my shame and feebleness.

SAMUEL COLERIDGE

☺ **LIVING THE HAPPY LIFE**

What is your favorite time of day to meet with God and meditate on His Word?

CULTIVATE WHIMSY.

There's an opportune time to do things,
a right time for everything on the earth:
. . . A right time to cry and another to laugh.

ECCLESIASTES 3:1, 4 MSG

Whimsy: It's usually defined as playfully quaint or fanciful behavior or humor.

How long has it been since you gave a tea party and dressed in a Victorian hat and vintage clothes? Or slept in the backyard in a tent, pretending to be on a safari? How long since you acted out your favorite storybook for your family? How long since you had a slumber party and stayed up all night painting your nails and braiding your hair? When was the last time you dressed in a costume for your favorite holiday?

You may shake your head at these ideas, but when was the last time you really had a good time and laughed until your sides ached? Everyone benefits from a playful spirit. Your light can shine even brighter when you express it with imagination. So come on, try one of these playfully quaint or fanciful, humorous ideas.

- Plan a Victorian tea party. Invite your friends to dress in clothes of a bygone era. Dress up your table in lace and use your best china.

- Call an old friend from your distant past and let him or her guess who's calling. Drop hints.

- Cook a special meal for your spouse. Set a beautiful table, light the candles, and turn on music from your dating days.

- Pull out those linens you're saving for a special occasion and use them. What occasion is more special than living life itself?

- Track down your old schoolmates during the holiday season and send them Christmas cards. Sign your first name only. Be sure to give a return address in case they want to discover who you are.

Treat yourself and those around you to a little whimsical living.

SIMPLY SPEAKING

A good and wholesome thing is a little harmless fun in this world; it tones a body up and keeps him human and prevents him from souring.

MARK TWAIN

☺ LIVING THE HAPPY LIFE

What one whimsical thing can you do today? This week? This month? Your happiness will grow as you take time out for fun!

SING IN THE SHOWER.

Worship the LORD with gladness;
come before him with joyful songs.

PSALM 100:2

The shower seems like the perfect place to burst into song. Secluded from the ears of others and enhanced by the echo effect of the walled-in enclosure, you can let loose and sing your heart out.

Absolutely any tune will do. If you don't know all the words, hum until you can fill in the blanks. Better yet, come up with something of your own. If you just aren't a spontaneous type of person, try a different theme for each day. Something like this:

- Monday—rain: "Rainy Days and Mondays" or "Singing in the Rain"
- Tuesday—travel: "I Left My Heart in San Francisco" or "New York, New York"
- Wednesday—love: "Only You" or "Have I Told You Lately That I Love You?"
- Thursday—animals: "How Much Is That Doggie in the Window?" or "The Old Gray Mare, She Ain't What She Used to Be"
- Friday—show tunes: "Hello, Dolly!" or "Oklahoma!"

- Saturday—fifties music: "Jailhouse Rock" or "Sixteen Candles"
- Sunday—worship: "How Great Thou Art" or "Great Is Thy Faithfulness"

The next week, change it up. There's no reason not to; the variety is almost limitless. Be warned, however: singing is contagious. Once you start singing in the shower, you may find yourself unexpectedly singing in the car, at your desk, as you jog, while you're cooking, waiting in line at the market, pretty much anywhere. When it happens, don't resist. Just let the happiness sweep over you, lifting your spirits and soothing your soul.

Singing, when you think about it, is nothing short of a total happiness-grabber! Sing on!

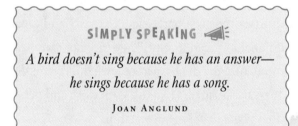

SIMPLY SPEAKING

A bird doesn't sing because he has an answer—
he sings because he has a song.

JOAN ANGLUND

☺ **LIVING THE HAPPY LIFE**

*O*nce you have mastered "the shower," why not gather up your courage and a few old friends and try out karaoke night at a local restaurant? You just might surprise yourself with your vocal abilities!

CHOOSE A HUGGABLE PET.

O LORD, how manifold are your works!
In wisdom you have made them all;
the earth is full of your creatures.

PSALM 104:24 NRSV

Our society has a passion for pets of every shape and kind: Some interesting. Some unusual. Some exotic. And some that are just right for hugging. Just about any pet will increase your happiness quotient—even watching goldfish swim around their bowl can lower your blood pressure and help you relax. But best of all are those wonderful, huggable dogs and cats.

Dogs are (for the most part) eager to please and capable of unconditional love and loyalty. They care not if you are rich or poor, young or old. Cats have a somewhat different disposition, but they, too, (usually) like to get up close and personal. Consider these benefits of pet ownership:

- Animals communicate through touch, emotions, wordless sounds, and instincts. Their meaning doesn't get lost in too many words, and they are incapable of using words to lie or manipulate. It's impossible to get your feelings hurt by something your dog or cat said!

- Animals are just animals. We don't place the same

expectations on them that we place on humans. And animals expect little of us other than caretaking and affection. They give us a pass emotionally—no work involved.

- Animals have a gift for tuning in when we're hurting physically, emotionally, or spiritually. They seem to know when we want to be left alone and when we could use a friend. They are there for us, but they never say the wrong thing.

We live in what has become a virtual hands-off society. Technology has made it possible to work at home, and it's possible to live in a neighborhood for years without meeting our neighbors. How gracious of God to provide us with such beautiful, adaptable, and pleasing creatures with which to fill the gap.

SIMPLY SPEAKING

Animals are such agreeable friends—they ask no questions, they pass no criticisms.

GEORGE ELLIOT

☺ **LIVING THE HAPPY LIFE**

Who are the pets currently in your life? If you don't own a pet right now, perhaps you could adopt a friend's to get a little weekly animal affection. Lots of love from a furry feline or pup is sure to make your happiness quotient rise!

EAT WELL.

All of us should eat and drink and enjoy what we have worked for.
It is God's gift.

ECCLESIASTES 3:13 GNB

Eating well involves more than just eating selections from
the food pyramid every day. It also means enjoying your food,
sharing it with others, and being thankful for the abundance you
have. Of course health issues are a part of everyone's life, but you
can still eat well and enjoy what you eat.

Make mealtime special whether you're eating with your
family, a group of friends, or alone. Take time to prepare dishes
that nourish the body but also those that make you and others
who share them feel satisfied and loved. Use tried-and-true
family recipes as well as new recipes passed on by friends. For a
change, you might watch The Food Network and try something
different for your next meal.

Create a pleasant dining atmosphere. Change the routine.
Use those special linens stashed away in the closet, light candles,
turn on soft music. Instead of serving your food on the same
old plates and platters, pull out the china your grandmother left
you or that stoneware you keep for special occasions only. Keep
conversation light and free of tension or confrontation; stress

hinders digestion. Those who sit at your table will feel special, but even if you're dining alone, do these things for yourself often.

Be thankful (see 1 Thess. 5:18). Saying grace isn't out of vogue. If you're not in the habit of saying grace at mealtime, you might want to start a new tradition at your table. A few simple words of thanks to God for providing good food are all that's necessary. You can even purchase books of prayers.

Eating well is more than a plate of food. It's enjoying that food and being happy and content with what's on your plate.

SIMPLY SPEAKING

A smiling face is half the meal.

LATVIAN PROVERB

☺ LIVING THE HAPPY LIFE

Good friends and good food are always an excellent combination! Why not invite over a few close friends this week for a home-cooked meal mingled with some great conversation?

FIND SOMETHING THAT AMUSES YOU.

Whatever thy hand findeth to do, do it with thy might.

ECCLESIASTES 9:10 KJV

Hobbies are a happiness magnet. Ask anyone who's pulling his vintage vehicle into a car show or fly-fishing hip-deep in a fast-moving river or placing an Indian head nickel into her coin holder. Hobbies can provide countless hours of relaxation and enjoyment, and they can be as unique and original as a person wants to make them.

The list of hobbies available is endless—knitting, collecting coins or rare books, cake decorating, kayaking, on and on. There is something for every taste, budget, schedule, and personality. Are you an active morning person with a surplus of energy and drive? Running might be your thing. Are you a night person who craves solitude? Jigsaw puzzles might be for you.

Here are some tips to help you find the hobby that's right for you:

- Choose something you feel passionate about. Don't try to impress or please anyone else. This is for you. Go ahead and experiment with different things you're interested in. You may try several things before you hit on the one you can get really excited about.

- Choose something affordable. Some hobbies can be so expensive that they can put you in debt or price you out of the game. Look for something that won't stress you out financially, something you can afford to do every chance you get.

- Choose something challenging. A hobby isn't supposed to be boring. Pushing through to the next level, finding that rare item, mastering something new: that's what a hobby is all about.

Don't waste another day. Get out there and find something, make something, do something! You'll be happier for the trouble.

SIMPLY SPEAKING

A hobby a day keeps the doldrums away.

PHYLLIS McGINLEY

☺ LIVING THE HAPPY LIFE

What are your favorite hobbies? Is there anything new that you have been eager to try? Let your creativity run wild and see where it leads you!

FINISH WHAT YOU START.

See that you complete the task that you have received in the Lord.

COLOSSIANS 4:17 NRSV

Nothing brings satisfaction like a completed task. Talking about it is much easier than the actual work, but talk only postpones the job. If you have trouble finishing what you start, here are a few pointers:

- Don't begin another project until the present one is finished. Too many projects at one time can be overwhelming and stymie your creativity.

- Break the work into smaller segments. How do you eat an elephant? One bite at a time. By breaking the work into smaller parts, you won't feel so overwhelmed each time you come to the table. You'll be surprised and pleased with each little accomplishment.

- If you don't know the next step to take, cast aside your pride and ask someone who knows. He or she will be delighted you've asked for his or her help, and you'll be relieved to find yourself moving on in the task.

- If you've lost interest in the project, put it aside for a few hours and take a break. Go for a walk, read a book, go to the mall, meet a friend for coffee. Come back to your task with a renewed spirit.

- Don't try to work too many hours in one sitting. Sessions that are too long affect the quality of your work as well as your body. You need to rest your eyes, hands, and back from time to time.

- Don't begin a project that you have no interest in seeing to the end.

Finishing what you start results in more confidence in yourself, knowing that you can tackle another project in the future with a clean slate.

SIMPLY SPEAKING 📣

An enterprise, when fairly once begun, should not be left till all that ought is won.

SHAKESPEARE

☺ LIVING THE HAPPY LIFE

Everyone has something on the back burner, a project that awaits completion. What's yours? What could you do to provide yourself with the motivation you need to finish?

LEARN FROM YOUR MISTAKES.

Who can discern his errors? Forgive my hidden faults.

PSALM 19:12

Did you pass the driver's written test the first time you took it? Many people don't. They go back and study the questions they missed and then armed with the right answers, they pass with flying colors. Mistakes don't tell you what you know; they tell you what you don't know. They don't show you what you did right; they show you what you did wrong. If there is any value at all to a misstep, it's that it's educational.

Unfortunately, we don't always learn the lessons our mistakes try so hard to teach us. Blinded, we stumble over the same obstacles again and again. We continue to make poor choices in relationships, finances, priorities. This happens because we fail to see our mistakes for what they are. Instead we dress them up with decorative touches such as bias, justification, blame of others, low self-esteem, a failure complex, pride, rebellion, rejection, and so forth.

For example, we refuse to accept that we are overweight because we eat too much—it's a thyroid problem or a family characteristic. We dismiss the idea that we keep failing in marriage, refusing to believe that we choose spouses who flatter our egos and prop up our insecurities rather than those who have strong character and integrity.

If you find yourself making the same mistakes again and again, ask God to help you break through the fog and see things as they are. Then your mistakes can begin to work for you rather than against you, warning you of danger, helping you to properly size up situations. Your mistakes can save you a lot of grief and bring you a lot of happiness—if you let them.

SIMPLY SPEAKING

Never let mistakes or wrong direction, of which every person falls into many, discourage you. There is precious instruction to be got by finding where we were wrong.

THOMAS CARLYLE

😊 LIVING THE HAPPY LIFE

Ask God today to help you learn from all of your mistakes, especially the ones you tend to repeat. Then be willing to make the changes necessary to succeed the next time!

STAY OUT OF DEBT.

Keep your lives free from the love of money and
be content with what you have.

HEBREWS 13:5

Nothing creates happiness like avoiding debt. And if it's too late to avoid debt, think how wonderful it will be to get rid of what you have: no more sleepless nights, no more slavery to your credit card bills, no more anxiety. Here are some tips:

- Make a spending plan. It makes your money behave. Include all essentials—take care of necessities first—but also allow for extras—those little things you really enjoy. Once you have a plan, work at keeping within its limits. After all, the goal is to stay out of debt. Exceeding your limit puts you in danger of acquiring the very thing you're working to avoid. Sometimes it's a matter of learning to be content with what we have until finances allow something different. (Read Philippians 4:11.)

- Allow for unexpected circumstances. Establish an emergency fund. Medical emergencies don't care about your budget. In fact, no one cares about the budget except you. Keep these items in mind even if it's only a small amount every month. Carrying these amounts over from month to month builds a reserve in case an unexpected situation arises. Some financial advisors recommend putting aside three to six months' worth of expenses, others recommend twelve months.

- Don't make a major purchase without thinking it through or at least waiting until the next day. Impulsive buying destroys your budget. Sometimes after waiting until the next day, you see that the item isn't nearly as attractive and the need for it isn't nearly as strong.

- Resolve to spend less than you make. If you can't pay for it today, you can't afford it. Otherwise, you're only increasing the debt load you're carrying.

Following a few simple guidelines can add years of happy, debt-free living to your life and will benefit everyone your life touches. That's a fact!

SIMPLY SPEAKING 📢

Poverty is hard, but debt is horrible.

CHARLES SPURGEON

☺ LIVING THE HAPPY LIFE

Experts say that one or two credit cards is more than enough. If you have more than that, consider pulling out the scissors and having a "cut-'em-up" party!

CONQUER PROCRASTINATION.

Commit your work to the LORD, and your plans will be established.

PROVERBS 16:3 NRSV

Procrastination is a happiness-buster and a time-stealer. It turns simple tasks into mountains and often results in inconvenience and unplanned expenses. The boxes of old books you meant to get rid of stack up in the garage, the food you meant to cook spoils in the refrigerator, the old clothes you meant to take to Goodwill pile up in the closet, the paint you bought for the house is still sitting in the basement. This is no way to live, and it doesn't have to be your fate. Here are some tips to help you get past the starting line:

- Make a to-do list and tackle it—one item at a time. A common mistake is putting too much on the list, so limit yourself to two or three items.
- Manufacture your own motivations. If your task is to clean the barbeque grill, invite some friends over to cook out later.
- Break big jobs down into manageable tasks and work on the smaller tasks in short intervals. Paint one side of the house each Saturday for a month. Tackle it early in the morning and then go do something you enjoy. If your

task is to clean the garage, break it down into sections and take on one section each Saturday.

- Take time to admire your accomplishment. Take a picture of the house when the painting is done. Pull up a lawn chair and enjoy the flower bed you planted.

Of course, procrastination can affect many other aspects of your life as well. Putting off renewing your driver's license can cost you a ticket. Putting off a physical can result in an expensive and painful illness. Add these to your list, get them done early in the day, and reward yourself handsomely. You deserve it.

SIMPLY SPEAKING

One today is worth two tomorrows; never leave that till tomorrow which you can do today.

BENJAMIN FRANKLIN

☺ **LIVING THE HAPPY LIFE**

What's the one thing you have put off today to do tomorrow? Put this book down, and go do it!

GO FLY A KITE!

If I rise on the wings of the dawn, if I settle on the far side of the sea,
even there your hand will guide me, your right hand will hold me fast.

PSALM 139:9–10

Nothing says happiness like turning your face to the sun and letting the breeze weave its way through your hair. Close your eyes for a moment and let your imagination take flight. You're in a beautiful meadow, the sun is shining, a red and yellow kite lies on the ground waiting for you to give it wings. What a wonderful way to get some fresh air and exercise while enjoying the outdoors.

Holding the string in your hands, you begin to trot. The kite rises from its prone position and trails along behind you. Then you feel a gentle tug as the wind catches your tethered bird and pulls it skyward. Slowly you permit the string to unroll from the spool, allowing the kite to rise higher and higher until it looks like a tiny butterfly floating in the air. At times it seems almost to disappear, but you know it's up there somewhere, because you can feel it tugging at the string, asking for more freedom. And you grant that wish because your spirit is up there among the clouds with the kite, soaring to newfound freedom.

Now imagine for a moment that you are that kite and God

is holding the spool. Sometimes He allows the string to unwind, letting you fly higher and higher. You may feel as though you're out there all alone in the wind. Then you feel a gentle tug on your heart and even though you may not be able to see Him, you know He's there.

It's amazing how a little thing like flying a kite can help your mind relax and your soul soar!

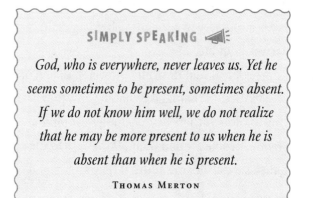

SIMPLY SPEAKING

God, who is everywhere, never leaves us. Yet he seems sometimes to be present, sometimes absent. If we do not know him well, we do not realize that he may be more present to us when he is absent than when he is present.

THOMAS MERTON

☺ LIVING THE HAPPY LIFE

Why not invite a few friends out for a kite-flying expedition today?

TAKE A STAND.

[Jesus said,] I know your deeds, that you are neither cold nor hot.
I wish you were either one or the other!

REVELATION 3:15

Happiness loves certainty.

People feel happier when they feel more secure, and part of being secure is a measure of certainty—holding definite beliefs and clear views about life.

Yet many people find it difficult to develop a solid opinion about the issues around them. Like chameleons, they "change color," trying to please others by matching the opinions expressed by the people around them. If they are in the company of liberals, they act like liberals; ditto if they are around conservatives.

They don't like to rock the boat, and they may even feel that they are being good peacemakers by fluctuating with every shift of the wind. But it takes a lot of energy to deflect and absorb all of those conflicting opinions. Is this your experience?

Maybe it's time to pick sides.

Start with something easy—pick a favorite sports team. You can see how a friendly rivalry can build camaraderie. Then move on to an issue of local interest. Will you sign that petition, or not? Will you honor the strike, write the letter to the editor, get involved? It's okay if you don't care to—that's an opinion, too—but do decide what you think about it.

Without being dogmatic and difficult to live with, you can be sure of what you think, decisive and informed. You can take a position and respectfully express your sentiments to others. They will value you more because you stand for something, and you will find that your faith is stronger, and you're more willing to share it with others. Taking a stand on a matter—matters.

SIMPLY SPEAKING

Christianity can be condensed into four words: admit, submit, commit, and transmit.

SAMUEL WILBERFORCE

☺ LIVING THE HAPPY LIFE

What is one issue on which you can stand firm?
Take some time and write out your position—it will help to solidify it in your mind as well as help you to explain it to others, when the time comes.

DECIDE WHAT YOU WANT OUT OF LIFE.

We plan the way we want to live, but only GOD makes us
able to live it.

PROVERBS 16:9 MSG

The reason so many people don't get what they want out
of life is because—drum roll, please—they don't know what
they want out of life. *Come on*, you may be saying, *it can't be that
simple*, but it is.

A story is told about a little boy riding in the backseat of the
family car. His constant whining finally reaches a critical level in
his father's ears. "What is it you want?" he shouts. The whining
stops for a moment and then the child responds, "I want to want
something." Sound familiar? We've all done it at one time or
another. We don't like the way things are, but we can't decide
what we'd like instead.

God has given each of us free will and ultimately control of
our destinies, if only we will use them. Do you want a happier
marriage? A better job? Whatever it is, go after it.

But, you say, I want to move into management, but it'll never
happen because I don't have enough education. Or I'd like to
start my own business, but I don't know how. Or I'd love to own

my own home, but I don't have any money for a down payment.

Keep making excuses and you'll never have the life you want. Instead of whining, enroll in night school, visit with a government business counselor, or open a savings account.

God wants you to succeed. He wants you to be happy and fulfilled and enjoying the life He's given you. He's ready and much more than able to help you anytime you call on Him. If you need wisdom, insight, guidance, endurance, all you have to do is ask. Decide what you want out of life—nobody will if you don't.

SIMPLY SPEAKING

Destiny is not a matter of chance;
it is a matter of choice.

AUTHOR UNKNOWN

☺ LIVING THE HAPPY LIFE

Make a list of the top five accomplishments you hope to achieve in life. How will you get there? What practical step can you take today to start moving in the right direction?

TAKE CARE OF YOURSELF.

All the law is fulfilled in one word, even in this;
Thou shalt love thy neighbour as thyself.

GALATIANS 5:14 KJV

"Giving no thought for his own safety, the soldier raced
forward, throwing his body over his wounded comrade. He then
lifted him onto his shoulder and ran back through a barrage
of enemy gunfire to safety." In time of war, these words are
truly heroic. They resonate with selflessness and sacrifice. But
war is an extreme circumstance, and these acts are uncommon
occurrences. In the crush of everyday life, we must give thought
to ourselves, or we will not finish the race God has set before us.

This may sound dramatic—after all, we're just talking about
taking care of ourselves. But it's an important concept that an
amazing number of people miss. It seems much more noble to
constantly be giving on behalf of others—to our own hurt. But
wisdom dictates just the opposite. You cannot give to others
when your well is empty, when you are exhausted, when your joy
is in short supply, when you are sick, and hungry, and hurting.
The Bible urges us to give from our abundance rather than our
neediness.

Before you begin your busy day, think about what you'll

do for yourself today: A long walk. A bubble bath. Lunch with a friend. A lost hour to read a book or take a nap. Taking care of yourself doesn't have to take all day. It doesn't have to mean a week away from your job or your other commitments. It doesn't have to be expensive or time-consuming, as long as it is something you will enjoy, something that will take you out of the range of responsibility for a little while. You'll find yourself happier and healthier as you get back to the job of caring for others.

SIMPLY SPEAKING

How shall we expect charity toward others, when we are uncharitable to ourselves?

THOMAS BROWNE

🙂 LIVING THE HAPPY LIFE

When was the last time you indulged yourself with some "me time"? As soon as your schedule allows, pencil it in. You'll be more refreshed and able to accomplish even more in the long run.

GUARD YOUR HEART.

Be ye therefore wise as serpents, and harmless as doves.

MATTHEW 10:16 KJV

Maybe you've had some friends along the way who weren't so good. You thought you could really trust them and open up, but you found you were wrong. Your deepest thoughts and secrets were exposed. Or perhaps you had friends who misled you. Instead of going the way you knew you should, you followed them and wished you never had. Maybe some so-called friend talked you into doing something you instinctively knew was wrong, while your heart screamed, "No!"

That's why it's important to guard your heart. Pay attention to that voice inside. If you ignore your heart, chances are you'll be risking more than you should. You are not obligated to share all your secret thoughts or fondest dreams with everyone, especially those who have not proven their trustworthiness. It's perfectly all right to say:

- "I'm not ready to share that."
- "That's between me and God."
- "Please respect my privacy."
- "Maybe . . . when I know you better."

And don't be dissuaded from that position by those who say:

- "Don't you trust me?"
- "It's wrong to hold back."
- "I won't tell anyone."
- "It hurts me when you refuse to confide in me."
- "God expects you to be honest and open about everything."

Your heart is the best you have to give to yourself, to others, and to God. As a wise woman was fond of saying: "It's foolishness to leave your most valuable possessions lying in the street." Your heart is your own most wonderful possession—treasure it and guard it carefully!

SIMPLY SPEAKING

Nine-tenths of wisdom consists in being wise in time.

THEODORE ROOSEVELT

☺ LIVING THE HAPPY LIFE

What are the deepest, most intimate secrets of the heart that you share only with God? Keep those things close to you—they are your greatest treasures!

TAKE CARE OF BUSINESS.

Diligent hands bring wealth.

PROVERBS 10:4

Some people love their jobs—some don't. Some people
find their jobs challenging—some don't. Some people like their
bosses and their coworkers—some don't. No matter where your
work situation falls into those equations, you can please God and
find a degree of happiness in your workplace. It's all about how
you approach it.

Too often we let circumstances at work dictate our behavior.
Your boss consistently dismisses your ideas so you stop
presenting them. A coworker gets promoted to a job you should
have been given so you slack off, reasoning that hard work
doesn't pay. The company you work for announces it can't afford
to give raises so you figure you don't owe it your best work.
You pay less attention and allow your work to get sloppy and
haphazard.

These are all short-term responses that won't do much for
the long-term happiness and satisfaction you want to feel in
your job. In short, they will produce nothing but frustration,
disappointment, and an erosion in your skills. Bottom line: you'll
make yourself miserable, and for what?

A better solution would be to do your job and do it well each day to please yourself—and your heavenly Father. Each proposal, each project, each big sale, each new idea, each and every contribution you make on the job should be marked with your own inner seal of satisfaction.

The circumstances in your workplace may be ideal—maybe not. They may change significantly—and they may not. That won't matter if you are taking care of business based on pleasing yourself and God. You'll have an inner happiness that even the boss's most enthusiastic accolades can't equal.

SIMPLY SPEAKING

It is not only prayer that gives God glory but work. Smiting on an anvil, sawing a beam, whitewashing a wall, driving horses, sweeping, scouring, everything gives God glory if being in his grace you do it as your duty.

GERARD MANLEY HOPKINS

LIVING THE HAPPY LIFE

What one thing could you change while on the job that would lead to a happier life?

PAY ATTENTION TO DETAILS.

The fruit of the Spirit is . . . self-control.

GALATIANS 5:22–23

It's amazing how a little thing like forgetting to pay a bill, record a withdrawal from your checking account, or put gas in your car can complicate your life and leave you frustrated. Yes—when it comes to happiness, details matter. And you'll be surprised how simple it is to avoid those unnecessary glitches. Here are some steps that will help you keep those little details under control:

- Put all your important papers in one place—a drawer of your desk or even a shoebox under your bed. When you need your passport, birth certificate, insurance policies, etc., they will be easy to find.
- Fill up your car with gas at the same time each week, even if it isn't empty.
- Keep all incoming bills in a basket on your desk and pay them all at the same time each week. This can be done easily online, but you can also do it by mail. Keep stamps and return address labels in the basket, and when you write the check, put it directly into the envelope. Write the date paid on the bill and then place it in its own file.

- Invest in a good spare tire, jumper cables, and a jack.
- Keep a calendar near the phone just for appointments. Every Monday, review what's coming up for the week ahead.
- Record your checks and withdrawals. Reconcile your checkbook each month with your bank statement.
- Keep a list of your medications, the dosages, and what they're for in your important papers box.
- Take your car in for routine maintenance every three thousand miles, or as directed by your owner's manual.

These, of course, are just a few of the ways you can manage your details, but they're a good place to start getting your frustration level down and your happiness level up.

SIMPLY SPEAKING

No life ever grows great until it is focused, dedicated, disciplined.

HARRY FOSDICK

☺ LIVING THE HAPPY LIFE

*I*s there an important detail in your life that you've been neglecting? Make the commitment today to take care of the little things first, and watch your frustrations disappear.

CHILL.

God's Spirit touches our spirits and confirms who we really are. We know who he is, and we know who we are: Father and children.

ROMANS 8:16 MSG

You've heard other Christians talk about their lives. Even in the midst of difficult circumstances, they maintain a simple inner happiness that you envy. You wonder why you don't have that same response to your faith and your heavenly Father. You feel grateful, of course. You know what God has given you. You're content with what you have—but still your mind and heart are unable to rejoice in it all. What are you doing wrong?

You may be mistaking devotion to God and the furtherance of His kingdom for an overwrought sense of responsibility. God has not equipped you to carry the world's burdens. You aren't responsible for the choices of others—only to share your story of faith in Christ when asked. You aren't responsible for the way things are being done at church—only to pray for church leaders, asking God to grant them the wisdom and insight needed. You aren't responsible for the condition of the world—only to be watchful and alert, praying for world leaders as God directs. You aren't responsible for answering prayer, that's God's job too.

That special inner happiness you've been longing for will

come when you chill out and remember who you are. You aren't
God; you are His child. You are right to care about others and
to work to live a life according to your heavenly Father's holy
commandments. But God is big enough to care for the world—
and to care for you. Relax and you'll feel the happiness bubbling
up inside.

SIMPLY SPEAKING

Do your duty and leave the rest to heaven.

PIERRE CORNEILLE

☺ LIVING THE HAPPY LIFE

The next time you begin to feel responsible for something
that is out of your control, stop and instead focus on what you
can do in the situation. Then, when you've done all you can
do, do something else! Take a walk, lie in a hammock, go bird-
watching—whatever helps you relax—and remember that God's
the One who's ultimately in control.

SEE THE BIG PICTURE.

Our light and momentary troubles are achieving for us an eternal glory that far outweighs them all.

2 CORINTHIANS 4:17

Life isn't fair, and it certainly isn't equal for all people. You may feel that you never get a break, that hardship and tragedy always come knocking at your door. Over time, your heart may have become frozen with resentment and even the dream of future happiness seems beyond your reach. Your only hope is a fresh perspective, a new way of looking at your situation.

For those who have no expectation of eternal life, the prospects remain grim. But for the beloved and redeemed child of God, this life is little more than a preamble to real life, eternal life.

Christ's disciples, in the early years of Christianity, suffered many hardships as well, many harsher than we will ever experience. They sacrificed their lifestyles, their property, and very often their lives but still remained constant and even joyful. Though they were beaten and imprisoned, their bodies burned and bloodied, they did not lose their faith. Why? Because they kept their eyes focused on another dimension, the big picture—life everlasting.

God does not promise that all will be well in this life. But He does promise to be in the boat with you as you navigate the choppy, storm-blown waters. And He also promises that one day you will know as you are known and see as you are seen. Then pain and sorrow will be no more. There will be no more tears. Peace will reign in your heart. Allow the hope of that day to nourish the tiny flower of happiness that longs to spring forth in your heart.

SIMPLY SPEAKING

Live near to God, and all things will appear little to you in comparison with eternal realities.

ROBERT MURRAY MCCHEYNE

☺ LIVING THE HAPPY LIFE

The next time you're having a "bad day," begin to think about heaven. Imagine the beautiful streets of gold and being surrounded by your loved ones. No pain. No tears. No stress. If you are a Christian, that is your future—the sorrows you experience now are only temporary.

DON'T COMPROMISE WITH EVIL.

[God] lifted me out of the slimy pit, out of the mud and mire;
he set my feet on a rock and gave me a firm place to stand.

PSALM 40:2

Some people make the mistake of thinking that they can
have it both ways. They can serve God but still dabble in the
things of the world. That's exactly what the enemy of your soul
would like you to believe. As long as he can convince you that
there's no harm in having a little fun—his kind of fun—he's got
you where he wants you. The simple truth is that you will never
be happy until you are ready to take a stand against evil.

Think about it this way: it's much easier to get dirty than it
is to get clean. Say you prepare for a very special evening. You
shower, put on your finest clothes, groom your hair to perfec-
tion. You look marvelous! Then, on the way to the car you walk
through a mud puddle. Your shoes are instantly covered with
muck and the hem of your dress or pants is caked with the stuff.
You might not even notice until you get in the car, but when you
do, the night on the town is over. You wouldn't think of going
on to your affair in such a state. You'd have to go home and get
cleaned up all over again.

God has saved you, redeemed you, dressed you in His

holiness. You are now the spitting image of your heavenly Father. But when you compromise with evil, it leaves a stain on your soul that ruins everything. Happiness is over. Your only option is to go back to God and ask Him to forgive you and help you get cleaned up.

Make no mistake, the pleasures of sin may offer you happiness, but they will not deliver.

SIMPLY SPEAKING

No matter how many pleasures Satan offers you, his ultimate intention is to ruin you. Your destruction is his highest priority.

ERWIN W. LUTZER

☺ LIVING THE HAPPY LIFE

*W*hat areas of compromise do you struggle with? Ask God to help you overcome temptation and never allow the enemy to gain a foothold in your life.

LEARN TO THINK LIKE A CHILD.

Anyone who will not receive the kingdom of God like
a little child will never enter it.

MARK 10:15

Jesus said some startling things to His disciples, things that must have set them back on their heels, baffled and amazed. Imagine how they must have felt when He told them they should become like little children if they wished to enter the kingdom of heaven. Can you hear the feedback? "What? Are You kidding? This discipleship stuff is serious business, certainly not suitable for children." It must have been tough for them to get their minds around the concept.

And yet Jesus knew that even the strongest, most reliable men and women could not carry the burdens that would be pressed upon them. His small band of believers would need to depend on Him completely, obey Him without question, and open themselves to a wide world of possibilities if they were to walk victoriously through the hardships ahead of them.

The child factor is just as important today. In order to receive God's help, you must be willing to see Him as your heavenly Father, trusting Him to provide all that you need and point out the right path for your life.

Give your life to God—every bit of it. He'll enhance the positives and guide you as you enjoy the good things He's provided for you. He'll also encourage you to place all your heavy burdens on His shoulders, freeing you to enjoy the life He's given you. All He asks in return is that you listen to His instructions and follow them to the best of your ability. Now that's a formula for happiness.

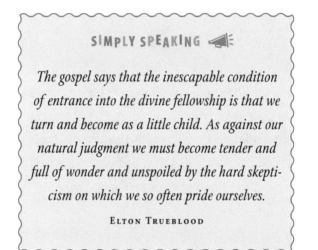

SIMPLY SPEAKING

The gospel says that the inescapable condition of entrance into the divine fellowship is that we turn and become as a little child. As against our natural judgment we must become tender and full of wonder and unspoiled by the hard skepticism on which we so often pride ourselves.

ELTON TRUEBLOOD

Close your eyes and focus on the happiest memory from your childhood that you can recall. That happiness can still be yours today if you come to God with a childlike spirit and allow Him to saturate your heart with joy.

PRAY, PRAY, PRAY.

Pray continually.

1 THESSALONIANS 5:17

Praying—it's as simple as breathing in and out. It's as natural as a conversation with a dear friend. And it's as steadily effective as the action of flowing water. To pray, anytime, anyplace, all you need is yourself and your God (who is always with you).

You don't need to assemble any special equipment or position yourself in a particular location. Even if you cannot utter a word out loud, you can conduct a prayer-conversation in your mind. Groans and sighs and smiles count as words in your prayer-conversation, and your body language is part of your communication as well.

Remember—prayer is a two-way conversation, not a monologue. If you pay attention, you will begin to learn what God's voice sounds like. You will experience the incomparable pleasure of His presence (sometimes in the midst of what may seem like incongruously unpleasant moments).

This is because, at its root, prayer expresses a love relationship. God is love. He loves you. He draws you to Himself. When you respond, the eternal conversation resumes.

It flows like a river, from adoration and gratitude through dialogue and discussion, to entreaty and petition, rippling with assurance and declaration, an ever-increasing intermingling of springs and rains . . . a life-giving stream, all the way through your days and nights.

Stay in the flow. It will carry you forward through work and play and crisis and celebration. It will keep you cleansed and fresh and attentive, moving on, night and day, through fair weather and storms.

SIMPLY SPEAKING

There is no thought, feeling, yearning, or desire, however low, trifling, or vulgar we may deem it, which, if it affects our real interest or happiness, we may not lay before God and be sure of sympathy. Our often coming does not tire him.

HENRY WARD BEECHER

☺ LIVING THE HAPPY LIFE

In your next time of prayer, try listening. Ask God to speak to you, and then sit quietly for five minutes, ten, even twenty. Who knows what He will say when you take the time to listen?

SEE LIFE AS A GIFT.

The earth is the LORD's and all that is in it, the world,
and those who live in it.

PSALM 24:1 NRSV

Have you forgotten again? It's altogether too easy to do so. It seems to be the default setting on every human heart—allowing routines and demands and obligations to supersede the fact that your life has been bestowed and is sustained by God Himself.

Stop a minute and think about it again, so you can appreciate it. Your life was not the gift of your parents or grandparents—all they did was pass it on to you. It's not a whimsical mistake, either. Your life—and all of life, everything that lives and reproduces—is a gift from your Creator-God.

He didn't have to do it, you know. Self-sufficient and timeless, He didn't need this green earth to be complete. But He chose to bring order out of chaos and light out of darkness. He chose to originate life, and He chose to share it. He didn't import life from elsewhere in His vast universe. He created it and He bestowed it. (What is life anyway, if not bestowed?)

God wasn't satisfied until He made some of it in His own image. You are written into that chapter, along with all the people who have ever populated this planet and will occupy it into the future, each life an integral part of the whole gift of life.

How easy it is to pay no heed to the Giver, the One who brought it all into existence and who sustains everything by the breath of His Spirit. How easy it is to look at our feet and see nothing but clay.

Today, look up. Remember. Acknowledge the Giver who is watching over you, His valued handiwork, breathing and pulsing and moving and thinking. As you exhale, smile your thanks to Him.

SIMPLY SPEAKING

All created things are living in the Hand of God.
The senses see only the action of the creatures;
but faith sees in everything the action of God.

JEAN PIERRE DE CAUSSADE

LIVING THE HAPPY LIFE

Why not write a psalm of joy to the Lord today, thanking Him for the gift of life He has given?

FORGIVE.

Be kind and compassionate to one another, forgiving each other,
just as in Christ God forgave you.

EPHESIANS 4:32

When *forgive* was a new word in what we now call English, it simply meant "to give." When you forgave, you gave or granted something to someone, or you gave something up.

The word wasn't spelled the same then, and over the years its meaning has changed along with its spelling. But today when you forgive, you are still giving something. You are giving up something too.

What do you give when you forgive someone? When you forgive, you give . . .

- your pardon, always.
- your pride, often.
- your promise—to allow the other person to go free from your judgment.

What do you give up when you forgive someone? When you forgive, you voluntarily give up some significant rights:

- your right to hold on to a grudge.
- your right to retribution.
- your right to be right.

It's not the easiest thing in the world to do. But whenever you do it, you will rediscover that forgiveness weighs in heavily on the happiness scale. As you place your pardon, your pride, and your promise on the scale, and then add to it your right to take it all back, the indicator needle goes higher and higher. More forgiveness proffered means more joy. That's what you get in return.

Granting forgiveness doesn't just happen naturally anymore than gift-giving happens automatically. It's an intentional thing to do, something personal. You consider carefully. You wonder if it's adequate. And then you go ahead and give.

Whether or not your recipient knows about your gift, God does.

SIMPLY SPEAKING

Forgiveness is not an occasional art, it is a permanent attitude.

MARTIN LUTHER

🙂 LIVING THE HAPPY LIFE

Whom do you need to forgive?

SEEK FORGIVENESS.

Blessed is he whose transgressions are forgiven, whose sins are covered.

PSALM 32:1

"Will you forgive me?" are four of the sweetest, cleanest words you can ever hear or say.

Unless the matter is a trivial one ("Will you forgive me for being late?") there are worlds of emotion bundled up within that short sentence. Sometimes that makes them difficult, almost impossible, to utter.

"Will you forgive me for hurting you?" (I know it was years ago. I just can't get it out of my mind. I have wanted to avoid you because of what I did to you.)

"Will you forgive me for letting you down?" (You trusted me, and I betrayed your confidence. I don't deserve to be forgiven, but I am asking for it anyway. I would like a chance to earn your trust back.)

"Will you forgive me for abandoning you?" (I didn't realize I was acting out of bitterness about having been abandoned myself. But that doesn't make it right. I was supposed to be there for you.)

"Will you forgive me for taking what was yours?" (Not only did I take it, which is stealing, but I lied about taking it. Now, not

only do I ask for your forgiveness, I promise I will pay you back.)
"Will you forgive me, Lord, for my sin? (Your forgiveness
means more than any other. Without it, I am lost. Please wash
me clean and keep me close to You.)

Yes. Yes, you are forgiven. Now you can go free. You were
buried in remorse, shame, and self-reproach. Now the sorrowful
emotions are transformed. Your spirit can rise again. Go in
peace.

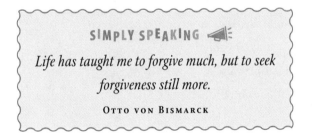

SIMPLY SPEAKING

*Life has taught me to forgive much, but to seek
forgiveness still more.*

OTTO VON BISMARCK

☺ LIVING THE HAPPY LIFE

From whom do you need to seek forgiveness?

UNLOAD YOUR HEAVY BURDENS ON GOD.

Cast thy burden upon the LORD, and he shall sustain thee.

PSALM 55:22 KJV

As you journey through life, is there a spring in your step? Are you smiling inside and outside? Or are you dragging your feet, weighed down with burdens, such as:

- Financial difficulties,
- Marriage problems,
- Health troubles,
- Difficult relationships,
- Worry about the future, or
- Too much work?

Are you wondering how you got here, so far from the ideal life you imagined? That question is for another day. Right now, the problem is that you are so overwhelmed that you are no longer able to enjoy your life. Burdens are giant happiness-busters.

The good news is that you don't have to carry your burdens alone. Really and truly. God Himself, who is bigger than the biggest burden anyone ever had, has volunteered to step in and do your heavy lifting for you. Starting right now.

Here's how it works. You surrender all your baggage—everything that has been weighing you down, stealing your happiness, and keeping you from doing what God has called you to do—and He will pick it up and apply His strength and wisdom to it. Your part then will be to walk alongside, listening to His voice, and doing what He asks.

You should know there is a tendency to take those burdens back. Resist the urge. God will do a much better job of resolving them than you will. And He'll let you know if there is something you need to do. Just relax and thank Him for the peace and joy you feel returning to your mind and soul.

SIMPLY SPEAKING

Why would you carry your burdens alone when God has so graciously offered to do it for you?

ANDREA GARNEY

☺ LIVING THE HAPPY LIFE

Take a walk today, preferably near a pond or body of water. As you near the shore, pick up some stones or pebbles from the ground. Begin to toss them into the water, and as you do, imagine that each is a burden that you have been carrying. Each stone that you throw into the water is a problem or worry that you have now turned over to the Lord—and He is more than capable of handling it!

SHOW MODERATION IN ALL THINGS.

Be well balanced (temperate, sober of mind),
be vigilant and cautious at all times.

1 PETER 5:8 AMP

Gluttony is an immoderate word. So is greed.

We limit the meanings of both terms. Too often we think of a glutton only as someone who overeats. Greed makes us picture a miser counting his carefully hoarded money, or a corporate mogul, driven by a desire to get richer. It's often not so easy to recognize the excesses of gluttony or greed in other matters of importance.

In every case, an immoderate absorption in a single thing to the exclusion of others keeps everything off-balance, and it creates an agitated, urgent state of mind. The driven person's mantras become, "More, more, more!" and "If only. . . ." and "I can't get satisfaction without. . . ." "I'll just play one more round and then I'll quit." "I'll just try one more store." "Somebody's got to do the worrying around here."

It isn't that money or games or shopping or worrying is 100 percent evil. The fact that there is usually something good about everything makes it easier to justify an overindulgence and more difficult to find the happy medium.

"Exercise is good, right?" Well, not if it consumes all of your time and deprives others.

"I enjoy hard work, even overtime." Yet you can't burn the candle at both ends indefinitely, or you will burn right out.

Do you indulge in some activity to an excessive degree? Is there something that you think about all the time? Maybe it's time to get a grip on your excesses (get outside help if you need it) and aim for moderation and balance in all things.

There's only one exception to the rule "Show moderation in all things," and that is in your approach to God. Forget about moderation there. Pursue Him with your whole heart. The more of God you have, the better—and the happier—you will be.

SIMPLY SPEAKING 📢

Moderation is the silken string running through the pearl chain of all virtues.

JOSEPH HALL

☺ LIVING THE HAPPY LIFE

*I*s there an activity in which you need to pursue moderation? Ask God to help restore balance to your life.

FACE YOUR FEARS.

Don't be afraid. Just stand still and
watch the LORD rescue you.

EXODUS 14:13 NLT

Fear can paralyze you—if you let it. But when you stand up
and face it, eyeball to eyeball, it dissolves. Why let fears steal
your happiness? Name them and then face them.

Fears have names: the fear of heights, fear of death, fear of
flying, fear of public speaking. You're probably aware of all of
these. But even the more subtle fears can be named.

For example, you may have a queasy feeling when you try
to reach out for your dreams or start on a new job. Stop and
evaluate your fear. Is it about the people you will be working
with? The people at home? Is it about God? Is it about failing?
Really narrow it down: *I'm afraid of failing at my new job.*

Now you are getting somewhere. In your campaign for
freedom, you have captured one of your enemies, and you have
obtained its name, rank, and serial number. Now you can face
it down. Ask God's Spirit to stand with you as you face your no-
longer-nameless fear. Then, order it gone and return your mind
to the business at hand. This may seem like a futile exercise,
especially when you have to do it over and over again, but slowly,

surely, you are gaining power over your fear and eventually it will disappear like smoke in the wind.

Fear is difficult to fight because it's a state of mind. But when you make it real, name it, face it, it becomes something you can fight against and win.

SIMPLY SPEAKING

There is much in the world to make us afraid. There is much more in our faith to make us unafraid.

FREDERICK W. CROPP

☺ LIVING THE HAPPY LIFE

What are your biggest fears? What can you do today to begin to face those fears and live your life in freedom?

REDISCOVER YOUR GIFTS AND TALENTS.

Every good and perfect gift comes down from the Father who created all the lights in the heavens.

JAMES 1:17 CEV

What was it you loved to do as a child? Draw pictures? Read books? Play ball? Go biking or swimming? Play the guitar? If you haven't thought about that in a long time, maybe you should.

Childhood is a golden time. Without the responsibilities and expectations of adult life, children are able to follow their natural bents. They act out of instinct, accessing gifts and talents hidden just below the surface. Close your eyes and think about it for a few moments and soon you'll see that those longings are still there. They never left, really. They just got pushed off the radar screen by the business of life.

You can rediscover your gifts and talents. It's simply a matter of looking past everyday life into the realm of God-possibilities. You say you're too old to be the ballerina you dreamed of being as a child? Well . . . no. You may not become the prima ballerina for a top ballet troupe, but you can rediscover your love for dance. Begin by stretching and getting into shape. Then dust off those pink slippers and sign up for a class at a local dance school.

Perhaps you dreamed of being president, but the realities of life led you in an entirely different direction. If you think you might not make it to the White House now, you're probably right—though stranger things have happened. But you can get involved in local politics, using your natural gifts of persuasion and public relations to make a difference in your community.

The gifts and talents God gave you are meant to be used. Whether that means planting and tending a new flower bed, building a table for your dining room, cooking a great meal, playing an instrument, or running in a marathon, happiness is there for the taking.

SIMPLY SPEAKING 📣

If you have a talent, use it in every which way possible. Don't hoard it. Don't dole it out like a miser. Spend it lavishly like a millionaire intent on going broke.

BRENDAN FRANCIS

☺ **LIVING THE HAPPY LIFE**

Why not make it a habit to try something totally new once a month or so? Spend a Sunday afternoon painting watercolors instead of watching football. Try your hand at writing poetry instead of reading a novel. You might just discover a new hidden talent!

DON'T PLAY THE BLAME GAME.

If we claim that we're free of sin, we're only fooling ourselves.
A claim like that is errant nonsense.

1 JOHN 1:8 MSG

In the midst of the throngs of people and the flashing lights of the great "midway" of your life, you and all passersby can hear the barker's loud cry: "Step right up, ladies and gentlemen, dissatisfied customers. Play the Blame Game! Surely you can find a culprit! Certainly it's someone else's fault. Just think about it! It's easy—by simply pointing a reproachful finger, you can divest yourself of surplus bitterness. What are you annoyed about? Do you want to blame somebody? Step right up. Ready? Take aim. Let 'er rip! Fire!"

Of course, don't step right up if you're not serious about this. Deadly serious. This game isn't for fun. Not at all. You aren't allowed to play this game with so much as a trace of a smile on your face. Look around you. Everyone who's playing the Blame Game has a sour expression.

Once you've played a few times, you're hooked. You keep playing it everywhere you go: home, school, work, driving down the highway, standing in the voting booth, or reading the newspaper. And that, of course, is the big drawback. This game perpetuates itself, and a chronically critical spirit has a way of curdling the milk of happiness.

Quite likely it's far better not to start playing the Blame Game in the first place. If that ship has sailed, ask God for His help. You'll need a generous dose of humility, especially at first, because you're going to have to take responsibility for your own blameworthy actions. But you have a Savior whose shoulders are broad enough to handle all the blame and shame in the world.

SIMPLY SPEAKING

*If you could kick the person in the pants respon-
sible for most of the trouble in your life, you
wouldn't be able to sit down for a month.*

AUTHOR UNKNOWN

☺ LIVING THE HAPPY LIFE

Have you ever played the Blame Game? Have you done so recently? If so, it's time to stop! Ask God to help you focus on your own strengths and weaknesses, as well as on what you can do to remedy the situation—not on what someone else needs to change.

MAKE YOUR PEACE WITH
THE BIG M—MONEY.

[Jesus] said to them, "Watch out! Be on your guard against all kinds of greed; a man's life does not consist in the abundance of his possessions."

LUKE 12:15

Maybe instead of using the dollar sign, we should start substituting a question mark. Why? Because it doesn't seem to matter whether you are affluent or impoverished, the mere mention of money raises uncertainties. Have you ever heard these questions:

- How can I protect my investments?
- Will my money be safe?
- What's the deductible this time?
- Who's offering the best interest rate?
- Just where did all that money go?
- Can I really afford this?
- How will we pay the bills?

Each question comes annotated with complexities and overlaid with reactions. The big money monster manages to dip his slippery green fingers into all of the nooks and crannies of our emotions. And surprisingly, greed is often a problem for rich and poor alike. That's why Ralph Waldo Emerson once said, "Money often costs too much."

If the high cost of your finances includes the sacrifice of your peace of mind, maybe it's time to start asking yourself some other questions. Whether your problem is too little or too much, start with these: *Is money too important in my life? Is it more important than my relationships with friends and family? Is it more important than my relationship with God? What can I do to get out from under the big M?*

Put your money in God's hands by creating a simple budget. Then pray over it. Ask God to provide what you need or to show you where to give or invest. He'll help you put money in its proper place.

> ### SIMPLY SPEAKING
> *Money never made a man happy yet, nor will it. There is nothing in its nature to produce happiness.*
>
> BENJAMIN FRANKLIN

☺ LIVING THE HAPPY LIFE

Budget—it's a dirty word to many people. But it's actually a simple way to add a giant dose of peace and happiness to your life. Make the commitment to create a budget and then stick to it. You'll be glad you did!

MARRY CAREFULLY—MARRY WELL.

Have respect for marriage.

HEBREWS 13:4 CEV

In this innovative, dynamic twenty-first century, some things have had to be sacrificed to make way for improvements. Marriage, for instance. Sure, in the past it was "till death do us part." But that was before we had so many options, wasn't it?

Now we can take more chances, because, well, there's always a fallback. Without raising any eyebrows, you can get a no-fault divorce, move to a new neighborhood, craft a new life. If this proves to be a less-than-happy solution, you can always locate a therapist, find a new job, or acquire a puppy. That should take care of it, don't you think?

It's a brave new world.

As it turns out, certain things haven't changed after all. Human nature, for instance. Cosmetic improvements do not seem to reflect much advancement in the condition of the fallible human heart. And since human marriage involves the alliance of two human beings, no money-back guarantees or lifetime warranties of happiness are being issued with new twenty-first-century marriage certificates. Although it is still very much a goal, marital bliss remains elusive.

Elusive, but not unknown. The one who chooses his or her partner with care will be rewarded. Two will be better than one. Through thick and thin, both of them will come home to happiness. They will never need to share their bed with regrets.

Marry carefully. Choose well. There is no greater happiness-buster than a bad marriage and few things that produce happiness in such abundance as a good one.

SIMPLY SPEAKING 📢

Two pure souls fused into one by an impassioned love—friends, counselors—a mutual support and inspiration to each other amid life's struggles, must know the highest human happiness; this is marriage; and this is the only cornerstone of an enduring home.

ELIZABETH CADY STANTON

☺ LIVING THE HAPPY LIFE

If you are married, why not write your partner an old-fashioned love letter today, reminding him or her of your heartfelt passion and love—including all the reasons you married your spouse in the first place? If you're not married but want to be, why not write a prayer to God expressing that same love and devotion and thanking Him that, in His perfect timing, He will provide you with the mate He has planned for you?

RECOGNIZE THAT IT'S A WONDERFUL LIFE.

The Spirit of God has made me;
the breath of the Almighty gives me life.

JOB 33:4

A great deal of your life may be behind you or you may have just begun to take life in stride. No matter at what point in life you find yourself, looking back with a skillful eye can fill the road ahead with happiness.

While you shouldn't linger there, the past has many lessons to teach you. In the best of times, it reminds us that God has poured out His blessings on us, allowed us to experience His favor, helped us to attain our dreams. He has been completely faithful, giving us more than we could have ever imagined possible. Remembering the good times also provides an opportunity to recall those who have given us good advice, encouraged us, and helped us along the way.

As we look back, we should also remember the tough times, the times when we struggled with emotion, issues of faith, and hardship. In the worst of times, we were reminded that God sustained us with His love and comfort. He walked right beside us as we traveled the path of pain and tragedy. And just like in the good times, He remained completely, unforgettably faithful. Remembering the bad times also gives us a chance to see the depth of kindness of those God has placed in our lives, confirmed the strength of our relationships, and given us renewed appreciation for God's amazing plan for our lives.

The happiness you seek may be just behind you. Turn around and take a look—just for a few minutes. As you do you will see things you missed when your step was heavy and your eyes filled with tears. Things you missed when you were breezing along without a care in the world. Take a look behind you— happiness was there all the time.

SIMPLY SPEAKING

Time is a three-fold present: the present as we experience it, the past as a present memory, and the future as a present expectation.

SAINT AUGUSTINE

☺ LIVING THE HAPPY LIFE

*I*f you haven't already, why not start a scrapbook of your favorite memories? Take a theme, such as "Favorite Lessons I've Learned" or "Those Who Have Influenced My Life the Most," and combine photographs and journaling to create a keepsake that will be cherished for generations.

BRING UP YOUR CHILDREN IN THE LORD.

Point your kids in the right direction—
when they're old they won't be lost.

PROVERBS 22:6 MSG

If you have children, you know how connected your happiness is with theirs. If your kids are happy today, Mom and Dad are too. It's circular. It follows that your children's happiness depends, to a large extent, upon yours.

Happy families don't just happen. They are intentional. And they aren't self-sustaining. As everyone grows older and circumstances shift, the circle can be damaged, and happiness can slip away.

The only thing in the universe that does not change is God Himself. He is an unchanging Rock. He is also the Source of all joy and all love, all wisdom and all patience.

He is the best Parent of them all, the prototype Father. His parenting goals are unqualified winners; they include trustfulness and obedience, stability of character, honesty and integrity, willingness to serve others, freedom of personal expression, and much more. God achieves each one of these goals in the lives of His children by means of His wise and loving discipline, and He provides rewards that are both tangible and intangible.

As we respond to our heavenly Father's care for us, we are better able to raise our own children. Along the way, we instill His values in our sons and daughters, and we find the day-by-day wisdom we need to be good mothers and fathers. There is no money-back guarantee, but it's the best deal out there.

Follow Him. Let Him be your heavenly Father. And raise your children to follow Him too. God will provide all the resources you need to get the job done.

SIMPLY SPEAKING

It is common sense to put the seal to the wax while it is soft.

ARTHUR JACKSON

☺ LIVING THE HAPPY LIFE

Start a tradition of family devotions in your household. Once a week, or even once a day, gather your children together for a time of Bible study and prayer. You'll be blessed for your spiritual commitment—and your children will never forget it!

BE A COLLECTOR OF PEOPLE.

A friend loves at all times.

PROVERBS 17:17

Stop for a minute and think about the people you've known in your life through school, work, church, community. Even if you're relatively young, you've met thousands of people. Many of them you considered friends. You did things together, laughed together, shared meals and secrets and daily joys and sorrows. Then you graduated, moved, or took a new job and those relationships just fell away. You didn't mean for them to, but they did.

Truth is, friendship is much too valuable to let it slip through your fingers, especially if you've made a significant investment in the relationship. You certainly wouldn't leave your other valuables behind.

A much better idea is to stay hooked up. This takes time and effort but the outcome is well worth it. You will probably have friends all over the country or even the world. Here are some tips to help you become a collector of people:

- Keep your addresses and phone numbers updated. This is much easier to do on the computer.
- Make that phone call. Distance may keep you from

visiting often, but long distance is relatively cheap. Call often and keep up on the news.

- Write letters. Written correspondence has a new name—e-mail. It's a wonderful way to keep in touch and you can send pictures.

- Pray for them. You will be forever bound to those you pray for regularly. Prayer is quite literally the tie that binds.

- Hook up as often as you can. Long visits may not be practical, but if you're looking for them, you will find thirty minutes in the airport or dinner at a trade show. You might even want to meet halfway for a day or two of fun.

When you make a friend, hold on tight. Friendship is something to treasure.

SIMPLY SPEAKING

Life is to be fortified by many friendships.
To love and to be loved is the greatest happiness
of existence.

SYDNEY SMITH

☺ **LIVING THE HAPPY LIFE**

What one friend do you regret having lost touch with? What can you do to reconnect?

LOVE YOUR WORK.

When God gives any man wealth and possessions,
and enables him to enjoy them, to accept his lot and be happy in his
work—this is a gift of God.

ECCLESIASTES 5:19

There is nothing more depressing than getting up every morning and going to a job you hate. Even a boring job can greatly decrease your quality of life. Of course, we've all had jobs we were obliged to take because of financial hardship or some other unfavorable circumstance. But that doesn't mean we should be bound to a life of work we don't enjoy.

If you find yourself unhappy in your work, it may be time to do something about it. There is a job out there with your name on it, one for which your skills and talents are tailor-made. It's only a matter of finding it. Here are some tips for discovering and pursuing the work you love:

- Think back to childhood. What types of things did you like to do? Were you a collector? An adventurer? In tune with nature? Did you enjoy taking things apart and putting them back together?

- Make a list of the things you really enjoy today. What types of hobbies do you have? Do you ever get so lost in a certain activity that you lose track of time?

- Ask others what they think you are good at. Don't complicate the question by hooking it to career, just ask them to give you their observations about your personality type, talents, and skills.

- Try a few kinds of work on for size. Volunteering is a great way to test your aptitude for certain fields. Do you work well with children? Adults? Outdoors? Indoors?

- Pray about it. God is anxious to reveal to you the person He created you to be. Ask Him to guide you as you seek your special giftings.

Work is a joy when it is compatible with your true talents and temperament. Don't live your life dreading tomorrow. Find the work you were meant to do and every day will be a delight.

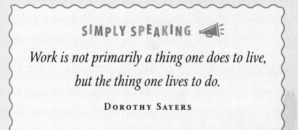

SIMPLY SPEAKING

*Work is not primarily a thing one does to live,
but the thing one lives to do.*

DOROTHY SAYERS

☺ LIVING THE HAPPY LIFE

What would be your perfect job? What steps could you take today to be able to land that ideal job in the future?

RESIST TEMPTATION.

If you carry burning coals, you burn your clothes;
if you step on hot coals, you burn your feet.

PROVERBS 6:27–28 CEV

Many times we fall into temptation simply because we don't understand it, we don't see it for what it is. The key to resisting is to pull away the beautiful gift wrap and expose it as an effort to realign us with our sinful nature and distract us from the things of God.

Jesus faced temptation shortly before He began His earthly ministry. The Bible said He went into the desert for the express purpose of dealing with the devil, making sure He was ready to stand up to the challenges ahead. After forty days of fasting, He must have been in His most vulnerable state. Perhaps this was meant to prove to us that resisting temptation has more to do with what you know than how physically powerful you are.

The devil tempted Jesus first with food, urging Him to prove how powerful He was by changing a stone into a loaf of bread. Jesus refused, quoting to Him from God's Word. Next, the devil urged Him to prove that He was God's Son by throwing Himself from the top of the temple. Jesus refused and quoted the Word of God. Finally, the devil offered Him power over all the kingdoms of the earth. Jesus was not fooled. Once again He quoted from God's Word.

Jesus was able to see the devil for who he is—a master deceiver. He gave no heed to anything he said, no validity to anything he promised. Remember that the only power the devil has over us is what we give him. Resist him and he will flee. You can bet your happiness on that.

SIMPLY SPEAKING

The best way to drive out the devil, if he will not yield to texts of scripture, is to jeer and flout him, for he cannot stand scorn.

MARTIN LUTHER

☺ LIVING THE HAPPY LIFE

The next time you face temptation, immediately bring the situation before God, asking for His help to stand strong and not give in. Your happiness—both immediate and in the future—will be much greater as a result!

VALUE LOYALTY.

Loyalty makes a person attractive.

PROVERBS 19:22 NLT

The concept of loyalty has changed in recent times. It used to be that people were loyal to their employers, working for the same companies throughout their careers. Companies were loyal as well, rewarding employees for faithful service and providing a secure livelihood. In our global economic market, these relationships are now rare.

Loyalty in friendship was once a given as well. Now we see it most often between gang members who vow to protect one another's nefarious criminal activities from police and rival gangs or religious extremists who will kill to express their faith.

We've distanced ourselves from loyalty and to our hurt.

Loyalty is a virtue, synonymous with the word *faithfulness.* It is one of the most important factors in any relationship. Without it, friendships are shallow, marriage is fragile, and business is unstable.

You have no real control over how the world operates or even over the way other people think. But you can value loyalty in your own life. Determine to be a loyal friend who keeps confidences and gives sound advice; someone who can be trusted to speak the truth; someone who will be there in good times and bad.

Determine to be a loyal employee, giving your employer your all, keeping company business within the company and always looking out for your employer's best interests. Determine to be a loyal spouse, being true in body and mind. Speak up when you see your spouse mistreated or maligned. Determine to be loyal to God as well. He has been loyal to you, vowing never to leave you or forsake you.

Value loyalty in your life, making it part of how you think and act in every relationship. Strive to be as faithful as God has been to you.

SIMPLY SPEAKING

Our loyalty is due not to our species but to God.
It is spiritual, not biological, kinship that counts.

C. S. LEWIS

☺ LIVING THE HAPPY LIFE

*W*ho is the most loyal person you know? How can you begin to emulate his or her loyalty?

LEARN HOW TO SAY NO.

All must test their own work; then that work, rather than their
neighbour's work, will become a cause for pride.
For all must carry their own loads.

GALATIANS 6:4–5 NRSV

The phone rings. It's your friend, Carol. She's in a bind. She
misjudged the time and cannot get to the soccer ball field to pick
up Tommy on time. The coach will be annoyed and inconve-
nienced. You're in the middle of making dinner, your husband's
due home any minute, and you've just lit the candles. What
would you say? What would you want to say?

Another friend, Trisha, stops by. She just needs to borrow
twenty dollars this time. As always, she promises to pay you
back, though she's never followed through. Your gut says no;
your heart screams, *What's wrong with you? Of course you have to*
help her! What do you do?

You run into your sister Susie at the store. She's got the
twins. You're hoping she won't ask, but she does. How can you
possibly say no—she's going through a divorce, all alone, and
you're the only one she has in all the world. But you've had the
kids every night this week. What do you tell her?

Saying no is difficult, but once you master the technique,

you'll be happier and much less conflicted. Begin your new lease on life by understanding that you are not responsible for other people's problems, lack of planning, or poor choices. This doesn't mean that you never help, but you do so on your terms and only when you feel you are doing more than enabling others to continue in negative behaviors. Sometimes it's an actual kindness to force others to get their acts together and act responsibly.

Get off the yes treadmill and never again allow others to steal your time and resources through guilt and a false sense of sympathy. Saying no is its own righteous defense.

SIMPLY SPEAKING
It is almost as presumptuous to think you can do nothing as to think you can do everything.

PHILLIPS BROOKS

🙂 **LIVING THE HAPPY LIFE**

*I*f you have trouble saying no, first practice saying the word in front of a mirror. Then start out small—with more trivial requests that occur every day. Eventually you will be able to say no even in emotional situations—and your life will be much happier as a result.

BE A TORTOISE, NOT A HARE.

I recommend having fun . . . experience some happiness
along with all the hard work.

ECCLESIASTES 8:15 NLT

If you're like most people, you find yourself running from
event to event, trying to keep up with busy schedules at work
and at home. The day is little more than a blur. You sense an
inner unrest and wonder about the happiness you thought would
follow your thoroughly modern life.

So many times we approach life as we would a race to be run.
The trouble is we never quite get to the finish line. We're like
dogs chasing our own tails. *When I graduate from college, I'll be*
able to relax. After the wedding, we can slow down. As soon as I get
this big promotion, I'll take a break. But each event reveals another
milestone for the taking and things never change. We keep
running and running and missing the point.

God intends for you to enjoy your life—not just the life you
have in the future, but the life you have now. Happiness is not an
imposing emotion. It creeps up only when there's a break in the
action. It needs time to germinate, time to release its essence.

That doesn't mean you should stop planning your strategy
for the next big hurdle in life. But as you plan, don't dismiss the

need for downtime—time to give thanks, time to reflect, time to rest your mind and body, time to enjoy your accomplishments, time to enjoy your life. Perhaps it's time to live the life of a tortoise rather than a hare. Keep moving toward your goals, but slow down enough to enjoy the view, appreciate the blessings, and warm yourself in the sunshine.

SIMPLY SPEAKING

I asked God for all things so I could enjoy life. He gave me life so I could enjoy all things.

AUTHOR UNKNOWN

☺ LIVING THE HAPPY LIFE

Why not remove one activity from your schedule today so that you can actually enjoy the other ones you have planned? Use the extra time to visit with someone or drive leisurely to your next appointment. You will arrive relaxed and at peace.

SATISFY YOUR CURIOSITY.

My heart mused and my spirit inquired.

PSALM 77:6

Why do people sit in a darkened theater, staring at a screen for two hours? They have to find out who won the war, got the girl, killed the victim. They want to find out where the treasure is buried, how the characters resolve their dilemmas. They're curious, and curiosity is a powerful force within all of us.

A strong sense of curiosity does more than motivate us in the movie theater. It urges us to reach out to others, explore the world around us, and find better ways of doing things. It's God's way of making us proactive, movers and shakers in this world.

Happy people are those who pursue the questions in their minds until their curiosity is satisfied. For some, that's studying why people act the way they do; for others it might be trying to understand why a tornado strikes one town and not another. It could be the impetus to so many discoveries. Through curiosity, God gives us the motivation to get to know ourselves, others, and the world we live in.

What are you curious about? Other countries? Other cultures? How things work? Just for fun, make a list of the questions in your mind, and then begin to systematically seek out the answers. What exactly is a quadruple toe loop? How do glassblowers learn their craft? What is that big red spot on Jupiter? It will be the beginning of an adventure that will change your life and bring you much happiness.

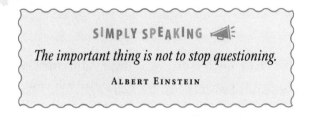

SIMPLY SPEAKING

The important thing is not to stop questioning.

ALBERT EINSTEIN

LIVING THE HAPPY LIFE

*L*ist five burning questions to which you have always pondered the answers. How will you go about satisfying your curiosity in these areas?

DEVELOP A SENSE OF JUSTICE AND FAIR PLAY.

What does the LORD require of you? To act justly and to love mercy and to walk humbly with your God.

MICAH 6:8

You may have noticed that we come into this world with a primitive sense of what is just, right, and fair. "That's not fair," is a statement children are prone to say as early as they learn to talk. That's because God has placed within each of us a conscience, a sense of right and wrong, a love for justice—not unlike His own. As we grow older, that sense of justice and fair play matures. And when it is turned over to God, it can become a beautiful instrument for the cause of righteousness.

A list of ways to live justly and fairly in our tumultuous world would hardly be possible because justice is a virtue that, to be effective, must be integral to every action we take. It must become part of our character. But there are some ways you can exercise your sense of fair play in God-pleasing ways:

1. Follow the law of love. In the Old Testament, a list of ten commandments was given for people to follow. Obviously, it was impossible to do so because everyone sins and falls short. In contrast, the New Testament tells believers in Christ to follow

the law of love. Through the power of the Holy Spirit indwelling them, they can choose to walk in love toward others (John 13:34).

2. Entrust your own needs to God. When you are treated in a way that you consider to be unfair, take your petition to the Lord and allow Him to work on your behalf. This keeps you from acting unjustly in retaliation (Proverbs 20:22).

3. Defend those who cannot defend themselves. Notice this injunction for Christians: "Religion that God our Father accepts as pure and faultless is this: to look after orphans and widows in their distress" (James 1:27).

Living justly makes you more like your Creator. It binds you to Him with golden strings. Make it a basic template for your life.

SIMPLY SPEAKING

Injustice never rules forever.

SENECA

☺ LIVING THE HAPPY LIFE

What injustices do you see in the world? In your own life? What things do you believe God is calling you to do to correct these injustices?

TAKE RESPONSIBILITY.

Be very careful, then, how you live—not as unwise but as wise.

EPHESIANS 5:15

Responsibility is a strange thing. Some people don't take enough and others take too much. It can be tricky to find that balance. But no matter where your propensity lies, you will be happier if you can learn to shoulder what's rightfully yours and step away from the rest. Here are some guidelines:

- Take charge of your own life. While you should listen to the wise counsel of parents, teachers, and others, keep in mind that the choices you make are ultimately yours alone. You cannot sustain someone else's vision for your life.

- Faith in God begins with a personal decision and continues through a personal relationship. There is no such thing as "family faith" or "faith by association."

- God expects His children (when possible) to carry their own weight, working and contributing to society to the best of their abilities. That means doing your best at work, at home, and as a citizen—no matter what others do.

- We must be honest with ourselves and others and take

responsibility for our actions, good and bad. There is no happiness in denial, only the illusion of happiness. When it bursts—and it always does eventually—it can be devastating.

- We are to love one another and one way we do this is by managing our responsibilities wisely. This is God's primary instruction to all His children.

It may seem like sitting back and letting others take care of things would be a great way to live, but experience doesn't seem to bear that out. Happiness comes as we shoulder the load God has given us and walk confidently at His side.

SIMPLY SPEAKING

Character—the willingness to accept responsibility for one's own life—is the source from which self-respect springs.

JOAN DIDION

☺ LIVING THE HAPPY LIFE

How is your responsibility quotient? Are you shirking any tasks you need to accept or taking on more than your fair share? A life of balance is always the happiest way to live!

CHERISH YOUR MEMORIES.

The memory of the righteous is a blessing.

PROVERBS 10:7 NRSV

Years pass so quickly. Your son graduates. Your daughter marries. What about the trip you took to Alaska with your best friend, the surprise party you threw for your spouse's fortieth birthday, your friend Bridget's last day at work? Every life has these little turning points, road markers along the way. You'll always have them in your heart and maybe even your head, but you can share them only if you take the time to preserve them.

These days photography is easier than ever and less expensive—even disposable cameras produce wonderful, high-quality pictures. Or you can use your cell phone. Isn't technology great? Whatever you use, make sure you have it on hand for every social event and capture all the memories you can. Think of each snapshot as the preservation of a moment in time: a crystal-line memory.

Film is incredibly easy to process these days, especially with the use of your computer, where photos can be downloaded, stored, e-mailed to friends and family, or printed on photo-quality paper.

Once your pictures are developed, choose the best for family albums. Make sure your album has acid-free sleeves, and don't forget to label them. Otherwise, you may spend the rest of your life wondering who that tall, dark-headed woman standing next to you in the airport is. Along with your photos, save other precious memories like ticket stubs, programs, and souvenirs.

Don't let your memories slip away, cherish them. Not only will they bring you happiness but they will also bring enjoyment to generations to come.

SIMPLY SPEAKING

God gave us memories so we could have roses in winter.

SIR JAMES M. BARRIE

☺ **LIVING THE HAPPY LIFE**

Why not begin a family photo album or scrapbook this week?

LEARN THE TRUE MEANING OF SUCCESS.

God rules: he brings this one down to his knees,
pulls that one up on her feet.

PSALM 75:7 MSG

If you live in the modern world for very long, it's hard to resist the pressure of the message of success. The message is not subtle, and it's everywhere you look.

"Get a bigger one" (house, paycheck, cheeseburger).

"Get another one" (car, appliance, college degree).

"Be strong."

"Get smart."

The message is reinforced at every turn, and it becomes the drumbeat to which an entire culture marches.

Step out of the success march for long enough to consider the true meaning of success. Take a long, hard look around you. Is it always the slimmest, fittest, strongest, richest, most beautiful people in the world who are the happiest? Or do the trappings of success sometimes become a trap? Look at the faces of the so-called successful—their real faces, up close, unretouched. Catch them after a long day filled with the frustrating ins and outs of striving to live up to their ideals of success.

Take another look around you. Introduce yourself to someone whose peaceful cheerfulness fills every room. That person may be on the bottom rung of the so-called ladder of success. Yet on the ladder of happiness, that person is almost touching heaven, radiating quiet joy. What's the secret?

Pleasing God. When your success rests in Him, you can no longer be manipulated by the pied pipers of this world. Instead you are motivated by the tender timbre of His voice. And you have all the resources you need to do the job He's called you to do.

Don't get swept up into the success trap. Put your success in God's hands and one day you will hear, deep in your heart, God's whisper of approval, "Well done, faithful one." True success produces true happiness.

SIMPLY SPEAKING 📢

A great many people go through life in bondage to success. They are in mortal dread of failure. I do not have to succeed. I have only to be true to the highest I know—success or failure are in the hands of God.

E. STANLEY JONES

☺ LIVING THE HAPPY LIFE

Take a moment and define what the word *success* means to you. How does your definition line up with God's definition? How can you alter your definition to allow for greater happiness?

APPRECIATE SIMPLICITY.

Let your word be "Yes, Yes" or "No, No."

MATTHEW 5:37 NRSV

Sometimes it seems as if human beings specialize in making things much more complicated than they need to be. Your grandparents used to have plain oatmeal for breakfast. Now your local supermarket stocks an entire aisle with an eye-popping variety of cereals, each claiming to be more "improved" than the others. Try to read the United States tax code (more than nine million words, sixty thousand pages, and growing more complex every day). Or consider the inner workings of your computer.

At the same time, we appreciate simplicity. In fact, people work constantly to reduce mind-boggling complexities to easier-to-understand components. To resolve knotty problems, we sort and simplify. We seem to be compelled to understand things, and the only way we can understand them is to find a way to make them clear and manageable. Aesthetically, we also find that we appreciate simplicity. Listen to these common statements used by real estate agents to describe homes: "Such simple, understated elegance." "Attractive, unpretentious, graceful."

God's creation is complex. He made it that way. And yet He has simplified it for us. You were wondering about the meaning of life? It's a mystery, is it not? Not when you're asking the Author of life. He says simply, "I am your life. Say yes to Me, and you will have it." (Read John 11:25–26.) He makes the important things straightforward and accessible.

Your life can consist of a welter of details, and at the same time, if you want to, you can walk with simple, natural ease. One step at a time. It's not complicated.

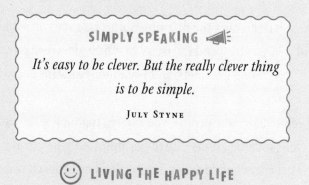

SIMPLY SPEAKING

It's easy to be clever. But the really clever thing is to be simple.

JULY STYNE

☺ LIVING THE HAPPY LIFE

How can you simplify your life today?

BE A GOOD STEWARD.

Think of us in this way, as servants of Christ and stewards of God's
mysteries. Moreover, it is required of stewards that they should be
found trustworthy.

1 CORINTHIANS 4:1–2 NRSV

Do you remember the first time someone gave you a dollar
bill and told you to spend it wisely? Maybe you were five years
old, just beginning to understand what money means and what
it can do.

If you're like most people, you carried that dollar around
for a while, looking for just the right opportunity to spend it,
debating the costs of things and the difference between what you
wanted and what you couldn't live without. That was your first
lesson in stewardship.

Most of us lose that magical appreciation for a dollar
quickly as we grow older. We often neglect to take the time to
consider wisely how our dollars are spent. But God expects us
to remember that all we have comes from Him and we are to
manage it wisely. He wants us to be good stewards—not just of
money, but of everything He gives us.

If you don't have a budget, it would be wise to make one, and
right at the top decide on your tithe for God's work—whether

that is a church building fund or an orphanage in Thailand. If you're listening, He'll speak to your heart and tell you just how He wants you to use it.

But don't stop there. The remaining 90 percent has also been left in your care. Avoid waste, live within your means, pay your bills, lend to those who ask. One day there will be an accounting—one that provides a reward for those who have been good stewards. Make sure you arrive in heaven with a prize.

> ### SIMPLY SPEAKING
> *There is no portion of our time that is our time, and the rest God's; there is no portion of our money that is our money, and the rest God's money. It is all his; he made it all, gives it all, and he has simply trusted it to us for his service.*
>
> **ADOPHE THEODORE MONOD**

☺ LIVING THE HAPPY LIFE

Investigate exciting ways to give to God's work throughout the earth. Sponsor a child in India or an orphanage in China. Support a missionary to Peru. Whatever you do, it will open your eyes to God's wider plan—and you will be richly blessed as a result!

TAKE HOLD OF GOD'S LOVE.

"Though the mountains be shaken and the hills be removed,
yet my unfailing love for you will not be shaken
nor my covenant of peace be removed,"
says the LORD, who has compassion on you.

ISAIAH 54:10

God demonstrates His unique and wonderful love for us each day. In our rush, rush, rush, drive-through, everything-in-an-instant world, we sometimes miss it and settle for the temporary substitutes the world offers, of which there are many.

Maybe you've been searching for love in all the wrong places, trying to get what you need from human relationships, money, possessions, popularity, or status. If so, your long, arduous search is over. You have an opportunity right now to reach out to the God of love who is reaching out for you. He knows you—even the you that you try to hide from everyone else—and yet He still loves you just the way you are. Every flaw, every blemish, every birthmark, every gray hair, and every wrinkle—He loves them all.

That's good news because it means no more disappointments, no more broken hearts, only a love as pure and reliable as the sun rising in the morning and setting at night. A love so strong that nothing can diminish its power—not even death. God loves you with a love that will last throughout eternity.

Won't you come to Him? Won't you take hold of His love? He's waiting for you, like a Father, arms open wide.

As He wraps His arms around you, you'll experience more love, peace, and happiness than you've ever known. Don't let this moment pass until you have taken hold of the greatest love of all.

SIMPLY SPEAKING

God's love never imposes itself. It has to be discovered and welcomed.

BROTHER ROGER

☺ LIVING THE HAPPY LIFE

You'll never know greater happiness and joy than what you experience in the presence of your heavenly Father. Why not take some time today to bask in His love?